COMBATIVES
FOR STREET SURVIVAL

HARD-CORE COUNTERMEASURES
for HIGH-RISK SITUATIONS

KELLY McCANN

BLACK BELT
B·O·O·K·S

COMBATIVES
FOR STREET SURVIVAL
HARD-CORE COUNTERMEASURES
for HIGH-RISK SITUATIONS

KELLY McCANN

Edited by Sarah Dzida, Raymond Horwitz,
Jeannine Santiago and Jon Sattler

Graphic Design by John Bodine

Cover Design by Kobranto Creative

Photography by Thomas Sanders

Demonstration Partners: Jack Stradley, Evan McCann and Marilyn Greene

Fourth Printing 2018

WARNING

BLACK BELT BOOKS
A Division of **OHARA PUBLICATIONS, INC.**
World Leader in Martial Arts Publications

DEDICATION

I dedicate this book to all the backyard, garage, church basement, firehouse and warehouse practitioners of combatives. Across the country, on various mornings during the week, people like you are getting out of bed slowly.

You sit up, swing your legs over the side, take a moment, reach for the Ibuprofen bottle and gulp down a couple—sometimes more than a couple. When you stand up or take your first step, you gasp as a previously unrealized injury makes itself known.

On the way to the shower, you notice a nasty scrape on your shin, bruises on your legs and welts crisscrossing your forearms. Catching your jeans on the floor with a big toe, you flip them toward the laundry pile and glimpse a blood smear near the strong-side pocket rim. You look down at your hands and think *Not mine*, then you wonder if it got there during the takedown-counter drills last night.

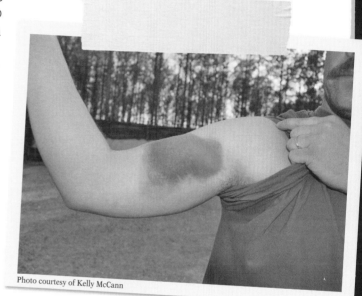

Photo courtesy of Kelly McCann

Twisting the shower control, it's apparent your right index finger isn't really where it ought to be. *Huh—how'd THAT happen? Screw it, it's close enough.* While the water runs, getting as hot as you can stand it, you step over to the sink basin and are startled by what looks back at you in the mirror. *How the hell did I get that peeper?* You look at yourself a moment then smile.

Good for you.

ACKNOWLEDGMENTS

T he guy appearing throughout this book with me is my longtime friend Jack Stradley. Jack's a retired, prior-enlisted Marine Corps Major who held billets (among others) as a Force Recon Marine, a counter-narcotics officer, a counter-terrorism officer and also as the Chilean Marine Corps Liaison Officer.

Jack and I met in the mid-eighties when he was the Commander of a Direct Action platoon. I was the Special Missions Officer for the Marine Expedition Force and responsible for training his unit to assume special operations duties. Part of the unit's training was a combatives program that I put together specifically to ramp them up quickly. We trained in combatives three hours a day, three days a week for three weeks—27 hours. The final combatives test was what I called "Styers' Alley" in honor of noted World War II-era Marine hand-to-hand combat instructor John Styers. Each prospective team member had to face 10 different attacks from Recon Battalion role players by repetitively walking into a darkened building. It was a simple "go/no-go" test; they had to resolve at least seven out of ten attacks within five seconds. The attacks were varied. A Marine's eyes might be "lit up" with a bright flashlight, robbing him of his night vision, only to be attacked while temporarily blinded by multiple assailants attempting to abduct him. Or he could be confronted with a potential threat to his direct front only to be attacked from the side with a weapon. It was a difficult physical test to say the least.

Jack went first, as leaders should. He handled the first few attacks well—all go's. His next scenario was *supposed* to start with a role player stopping him to ask a question. Stradley would likely take a step back to gain some space and assess the threat, hands up in a nonthreatening manner. When the role player saw Jack step back, he was supposed to try to sucker punch him. Except the role player was a huge, not terribly adept role player. Being a little nervous about getting it right, he didn't. As soon as the role player got in front of Jack, he just suckered him forgetting the, ah, question part.

Stradley took the shot square in the face; I'd have dropped like a stone. He stumbled back, and I thought he was buckling. Then, as sometimes happens, Jack came back to life pissed. It took three men to pull Jack off the role player that he had knocked down and was on the way to knocking out. Stradley made his bones with me right there.

He's always up for anything, never complains and gets after it pretty damn well himself. From the time we were in the Corps together and still today, he's had my back, and I've had his more than once—and I'm not talking about *jiu-jutsu*.

Thanks, Jack.

I'd also like to give special thanks to U.S. Marine Raider Jim Smith and U.S. Army Ranger Ed Turner—two World War II veterans who epitomize what this book is all about.

PREFACE

Before the movie *Fight Club* came out in 1999, I ran one. It wasn't my idea; an old Executive Officer of mine from the Marine Corps had asked, "Why don't you do some combatives training for regular guys?"

I dismissed the idea, telling "Big George" that regular Joes wouldn't subject themselves to that kind of abuse. He shrugged and, without expression, said, "I would." Big G was around 50 years old at the time, had seen extensive combat in Vietnam and weirdly had been shot more times out of combat than in. He also was (and still is) a wild ass.

"Like who?" I asked.

Big George replied, "I dunno. Guys we know that would wanna bang."

Since I'd gotten out of the Corps four years earlier, I'd been training special-operations personnel every day for a living. Always up for a good time and more training, I finally agreed to Big George's suggestion.

We met every Thursday night at a local firehouse with the permission of the Lieutenant, who was a neighbor of mine. I'm sure the county had *no* idea what was going on—the implied liability of what we were doing would've made it impossible for any county official to condone our use of a government building. I didn't care about the liability and neither did my neighbor or any of the men and women who showed up to train. You had to be vouched for by an existing member to join, and if any FNG (Fucking New Guy) screwed the pooch, whoever vouched him in never lived it down.

We trained on the concrete floor in street clothes. Whenever an FNG showed up, he or she was just thrown into the mix. It didn't matter what we were doing that night, they were doing it, too.

I taught the group the same techniques I taught my special-operations students, excluding "tradecraft" content like apprehension avoidance or restraint release. We gave no quarter, and best of all, no one expected any.

This was years before the "reality-based" craze started. Thursday nights sometimes got as amped as street fighting. We trained in bathroom stalls, stairwells and between parked cars. I'd have the volunteer firemen move the trucks out of the bay and turn the overhead lights out, or turn on their emergency vehicles' strobe lights and sirens, or sometimes use a single spotlight to light the bay we used for training. We'd wipe our forearms with baby oil to simulate the slipperiness of blood while practicing knife-countering and knife-on-knife drills. Our stick training culminated with monthly full-contact fights using rattan sticks. We only wore street hockey helmets, gloves and lacrosse elbow pads for protection. (Go Dog Brothers![1])

Unapologetically, learning to prevail in street violence isn't pain free; you pay by enduring self-imposed physical punishment. There's no way to achieve the skill, develop the courage or grow the hunger to survive a violent attack without training hard. That's the price, and people from all walks of life showed up at the firehouse to pay it. There wasn't a Thursday night someone didn't get cut, get a sprain or get kicked in the balls hard enough to make them puke. It was great.

Black belts with years of experience were beaten and manhandled by guys who'd been training for only months. Often they would remark exuberantly, "Man, this is what I thought I'd get from martial arts!" They never returned to their *dojo*. This happened so often that, after a couple of years,

---

[1] Dog Brothers is a full-contact stick-fighting organization.

Photos courtesy of Kelly McCann

the converts suggested a "black belt burning." So one weekend, standing around a burn barrel while drinking beer, in went the certificates, the belts and the trappings of traditionalism.

In our litigious society, I doubt it's possible to make a commercial school for combatives work. Even in the military, it was a constant battle to "keep it real" because a soldier or Marine injured in training is "combat ineffective." He was off the active rolls temporarily, and this diminishes unit end strength.

Personally, I think *real* combatives are best kept underground. If you agree, then you've taken the best first step by buying this book. Your next step is to find some like-minded friends, who can take as much punishment as they can give, and start training together. Grass-roots groups avoid a lot of bullshit because there's no organization (read "unnecessary structure") getting in the way. As an analogy, I know a lot of spiritual people who insist they don't need a minister or church and don't want to deal with a congregation—get my drift?

You don't have to share my minimalist philosophy or believe in my approach to training for true street effectiveness. You can do everything in this book, some of it or none because how you develop your combatives skills is your business. I'm just happy you were open-minded enough to read it.

Like anyone, I'm a victim of my own experiences. Mine have resulted in becoming intimately familiar with both foreign and domestic attackers and their methods of attack. I've learned what it takes to prevail on the street where fights are unpredictable and comprise the unregulated use of force by unskilled, vicious attackers—criminals who could care less if their victims survive or not.

I don't claim combatives are a panacea in this book. There isn't *any* martial magic that guarantees victory. Spock's Vulcan neck pinch is every bit as fictional as the bullshit "no-touch" knockout techniques or other wacky crap that spins around in the martial ether. I know this as a skeptic, as a cynic and through personal experience.

For example, while serving with a special-missions unit in the late '80s, I trained daily with a dedicated martial artist. He held ranks in more martial arts than I knew how to pronounce, and some were pretty arcane. The day he retired, he caught up with me at the gym before we both went to his farewell ceremony.

Smiling, he said, "I couldn't think of a more fitting thing to do than spend my last couple of hours at the unit fighting with you." So we fought, as we'd done countless times before. He was a skilled, tough bastard with as high a pain threshold as I've ever encountered. As we were winding down our workout, he began to tell me about some fairly esoteric *aikijujutsu* techniques he had finally mastered. Some, he claimed, resulted in knockouts, while others purportedly threw people to the ground without apparent physical effort.

Wrinkling my brow, I didn't say anything. He was a senior officer; I was a Major, and he was a full Colonel. He looked at me and asked, "What?"

As happens in many SMUs, we'd known each other for years, were on a first-name basis and had become training partners and friends. Again, he asked, "What?"

"You know I don't believe in that shit," I said.

"Well, let me show you," he replied.

I quickly agreed, and he was equally quick to say, "Now, I don't know what this will do to you. Are you *sure* you're OK with me doing this?"

"Yup."

"I'm not sure how much control I have over it so…."

"Jeeeeeezus," I said, "Just do it already, will you?"

And he did. But nothing happened. So he did it again. Still nothing.

"What do you feel?" he asked.

"Nothing," I answered.

And so it went. I didn't fall down, get dizzy or feel nauseated. He couldn't magically throw me to the ground or make me feel weak in the knees and faint. Eventually he grew frustrated, and the situation became awkward even for longtime friends.

"Screw it man," I said to break the tension. "You know us Marines—thickheaded, sloe-eyed, knuckle-draggers…maybe I'm just impervious to it."

"Fucking Marines!" he said in exasperation. Shaking his head, he laughed and slapped my shoulder. Together, we walked off the mat.

My point is you owe it to yourself to be a skeptic about all techniques and those who teach them. The old cliché "seeing is believing" doesn't apply to combatives. Feeling is believing. Doing is believing. Unless you've felt a technique, done it to someone *and* achieved satisfactory results, you shouldn't believe in it.

Listen, ads claiming you'll be taught "secret" techniques known only to the art's masters are an insult to your intelligence. Anyone claiming their five-minute class will enable you to beat any street fighter is LYING. Instructors who are intentionally unclear about their background or experience and claim "secret" status with some unnamed organization are charlatans. Any claims of a classified curriculum are ludicrous. That's why it's important to be your own judge and judge wisely.

Combatives techniques aren't innumerable, intricate or nuanced. They're not so difficult that only octogenarian grandmasters can fully understand or be proficient in them. Combatives techniques aren't about finesse. It's unlikely you'll have an "a-HA" moment while looking over the techniques in this book. Combatives are not elegant, mysterious, esoteric or sophisticated. They're simply the analogous equivalent of a wrecking ball—when swung hard, shit gets broken.

Mastering combatives doesn't guarantee you'll win a fight anymore than mastering *kempo*, *taekwondo*, *jeet kune do* or *jiu-jitsu* does. Street violence is wildly unpredictable. Skill is only part of the equation for success. I was reminded of this recently when I served as a subject-matter expert for the defense at a murder trial in Northern Virginia. The defendant was a 23-year-old kid (5 feet 10 inches tall and 175 pounds) who killed a 40-year-old felon (6 feet 2 inches tall and 230 pounds).

I used the autopsy reports and photos to reconstruct the stabbing on a training mannequin by piercing the torso at the correct anatomical points and angles. Based on the placement and tapered appearance of the wounds, it was obvious the felon had initially been the aggressor.

He'd beaten down the kid, which prevented any escape. Believing he was going to be beaten to death, possessing no fight skills and seeing no alternative, the kid pulled out his folding knife and slashed at his attacker. He blindly stabbed the attacker's torso four times—end of story. Despite having been fatally stabbed, the felon kept pummeling the kid (probably thinking he had only been punched) until he started to bleed out. Afterward, the coroner found more than 500 cubic centimeters of blood in the decedent's stomach and even more in his thoracic cavity.

The markers replicate the knife wounds sustained by the decedent.

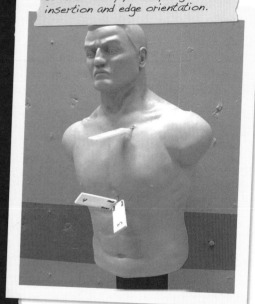

Photos courtesy of Kelly McCann

Each of the markers was inserted to accurately portray angle of insertion and edge orientation.

I'm sure the felon was convinced he was winning and that he could beat on his smaller, weaker and less fearsome victim at will—right up to the point he fell dead on the ground. I'm pretty sure he died bewildered without actually understanding how the confrontational dynamic reversed so quickly. My point is you never know who the person you're fighting is and what they either *may* be or *are* capable of.

For that reason (and others that will become increasingly more obvious as you read), the primary theme woven throughout this book is to assiduously avoid confrontation. By the time you finish reading it, the many reasons should be crystal clear.

The secondary theme is if you can't avoid or escape a fight, prevail in it. My dad taught me the only dirty fight is the one you lose. A criminal has no intention of being fair when he attacks you. He'll do anything to punk you, leaving you down and out. Fighting him restrained by some self-imposed fantasy of fair fighting is stupid and likely to get you seriously injured or killed. You can't practice combatives if you don't cultivate the right attitude.

Combatives are easily learned, quickly recalled under duress and devastatingly effective when applied with the right mind-set and violence of action, but the most powerful weapon you have is your brain. Use it so you don't *have* to fight.

Thanks for thinking there's value in what I teach and buying this book. I hope you learn something, get a few laughs and thoroughly enjoy it. Now go get some Ibuprofen and bandages and get busy!

—Kelly McCann
2009

TABLE OF CONTENTS

TABLE OF CONTENTS

TABLE OF CONTENTS

PART I

COMBATIVES ARE A ONE-SIDED STORY.

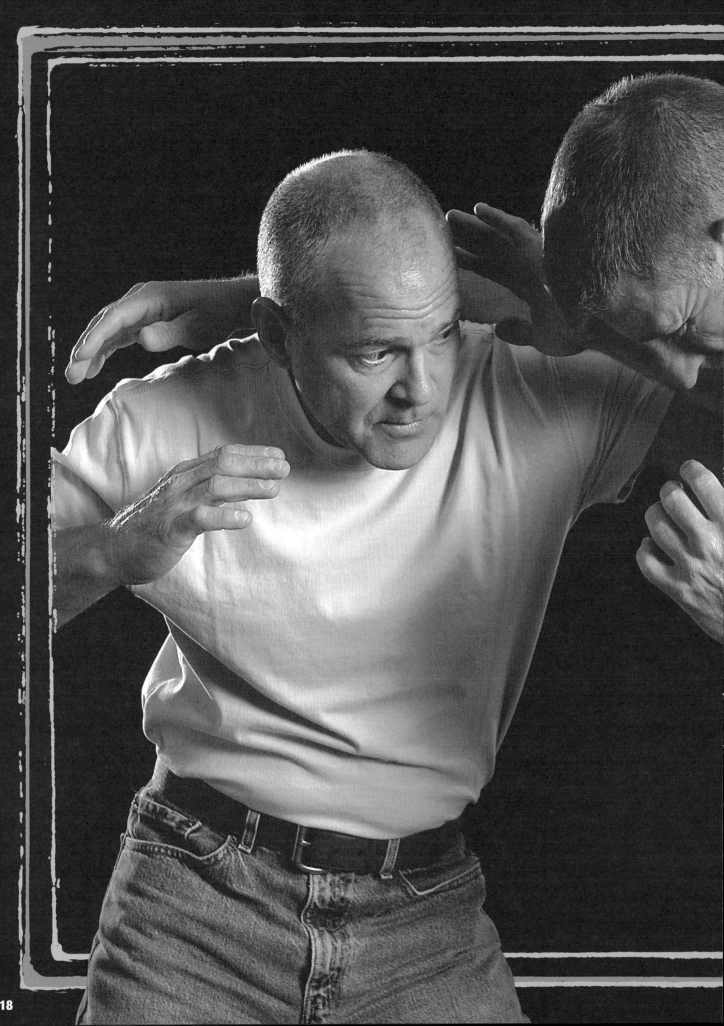

CHAPTER 1
WHAT ARE COMBATIVES?

Combatives (\kəm-ˈba-tivz\)

n: a set of personal combat principles applied to an intentionally limited number of simple (predominantly Western) self-defense and fighting techniques that are easily recalled under duress and able to be linked, creating short combative sequences.

That's my definition. Combatives are self-defense concision. Traditionally practiced in the military, combatives have been embraced by civilians because, although violent, when your life is threatened it's your right to defend yourself as quickly as possible by any means necessary. Combatives meet those requirements.

Life-taking is life-taking no matter whether it's on a battlefield or in Boston. Combatives are explosively violent, but contrary to popular misconception, they do conform to a legitimate force continuum, which is a progression of force values indicating how much force is legally appropriate given increasingly threatening situations. Generally, combatives focus much more heavily on significant and lethal physical threats.

Combatives were conceived to provide massive numbers of infantrymen reliable techniques of personal combat that don't:

- require an inordinate amount of time to learn and master
- demand extraordinary strength or athleticism
- rely on inordinate flexibility

Combatives aren't complicated or heavily stylized. They're distilled to the bare essentials, so each technique is simple to recall and execute under duress in disadvantageous environmental conditions.

The following anecdotes exemplify how chaotic life and death struggles are and why self-defense techniques must be brutal and simple:

Story One

Before I went on active duty in the Marine Corps as a young man, I had an intimate conversation with my uncle, John Pelletier, a World War II Marine who fought at Iwo Jima and in other epic Pacific theatre battles. He won the Bronze Star, was awarded the Purple Heart and left the Marine Corps wearing the rank of Sergeant.

He invited me down from college to congratulate me on graduating, being commissioned in the Corps and to give me "the gouge"—Marine-speak for the "lowdown" on what to expect—in my new career. At the time, he was the Chief of Police in Merrimack, New Hampshire.

We were well into a bottle of something, chasing it with Budweisers, when he disappeared for a moment only to return with his KaBar combat knife. The sheath and leather spacer handle were dark brown. The brass snap had a waxy, green-blue corrosion where it touched the leather.

John was known as a tough bastard not prone to sentimental moments. Once in the 1970s, he'd loaded 20 of his police officers onto a school bus to face down a notorious outlaw motorcycle gang causing problems at a New Hampshire racetrack. He stopped the bus driver at a local hardware store on the way and bought Hickory ax handles for all his men. When they arrived at the track, John ordered his men to fall into formation. He searched out the outlaw leader and gave the man a choice—leave town or be "tuned up" by him and his Hickory-wielding men, then arrested. The gang left immediately.

My uncle's issued USMC KaBar knife. "I want you to have this," he said, handing me the knife. "I carried it through the war."

As I picked up the knife, it hit me where this knife had been and under what conditions it had been carried.

"So what was closing with the enemy like?" I asked. "I mean, how did it sort out on the battlefield? How'd you pick a particular Jap to go after, and how did each of them target a Marine?"

Johnny picked up his glass and looked away, clearing his throat. "It's not like that; it's a collision. It's like the worst goddamned bar fight you can imagine—but to the death. It's chaos. Two Jarheads would grab a Jap, and then a third might notice and hit the Jap in the head with a Garand or an entrenching tool. Maybe one of the Marines would get bayoneted, but before the Jap could take his bayonet out, another Marine would bayonet him. It was crazy; wasn't orderly—didn't make sense."

Johnny took a drink. "I remember being nervous before they'd come. I remember my hands would shake afterward. But I don't remember anything during those fights except how pissed off I was. I hated those Japs because they were our enemy and not because they were soldiering; we were too. I think I probably hated them because they made me feel angry and scared. Anyone who says they aren't is lying or a nut. You just gotta use all that emotion to your advantage and let it go. It's a vicious, vile, goddamned thing—a wild-ass scramble."

Whoa. Having leaned forward to hear his answer, the only sound I could hear was a housefly bumping into the overhead light shade. What the hell do you say to that? It was sobering stuff for a 21-year-old to hear.

Story Two

In the 1990s, a couple years after I left the Corps, I was invited back to participate as a subject-matter expert in a review of the close-combat program in Quantico, Virginia.

Attending the panel at my invitation was Jim Smith, a World War II veteran. He had enlisted in the Marine Corps in 1939 and initially served in Cuba. In March 1942, he was assigned to the First Marine Raider Battalion. As a Raider, he participated in the battles of Tulagi, Tasimboko and Guadacanal and in the two battles at Matanikau River. He was awarded the Silver Star for action in Tulagi, a Gold Star in lieu of a second Silver Star Medal for actions in the Battle of the Ridge on Guadacanal, and the Purple Heart. He went on to serve in the CIA from 1952 to 1979. Jim is just something else (and still shoots, by the way).

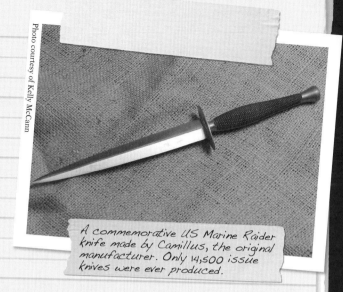

A commemorative US Marine Raider knife made by Camillus, the original manufacturer. Only 14,500 issue knives were ever produced.

He looks like a gregarious grandfather; he actually is a gregarious grandfather—wears a big, bushy white mustache, is quick with a smile and as genuine a man as I'm likely to ever meet. I worked with him frequently, training intelligence personnel in advanced concealed pistol skills and unarmed combat at a commercial training site near Williamsburg, Virginia. He was the program manager of a special surveillance detection unit and I was their Chief Instructor.

During the weeklong SME conference, a Staff Sergeant—whose complete combatives experience was solely based on what he had learned in the Marines—was really vocal about promoting some idea or another of his as an absolute necessity to the program. He was young, inexperienced and defensive because he was in a room surrounded by subject-matter experts with far more experience.

Jim probed him with a question, which the young Staff Sergeant mistook as a challenge, compelling him to ratchet up his argumentative tone. But Jim didn't take the bait, and soon the conversation digressed into a question about improvised weapons on the battlefield. Jim listened awhile and asked, "Any of you know what the best improvised hand-to-hand weapon is?" The conversation died down, and everyone looked at him.

His voice quieted when he said, "The Corpsman's hatchet."

He had everyone's attention and went on:

"The Corpsman's hatchet was the best damn hand-to-hand weapon you could grab. The Raider knife was terrible. We all thought the Fairbairn-Sykes-based design[2] was useless—tips broke off all the time, the rounded handle rolled in your hand and was hard to hang onto when it got wet. Totally useless. But that friggin' hatchet went through men like butter." Jim's voice rose and so did he. He looked around the conference table.

"That goddamned thing handled and swung like a dream. It'd pierce a helmet or split a breastbone. If you could get your hands on the Corpsman's hatchet, you were good to go." He sat down. There was silence.

Who cares if the Marine Corps didn't use Corpsman's hatchets anymore? It was the way Jim had stated his belief that silenced the room. Here was a guy who looked like a kindly old grandfather, and at one time in his life, he'd held a hatchet in his hand and cleaved an enemy's head open with it. He'd planted it in some poor bastard's chest and then anxiously looked for another place to stick it.

It was the sheer violence in his words that was the stunner—Jim's resolute commitment to kill some Bushido-believing bastard with nothing more than a hatchet in his hand.

---

[2] The Fairbairn-Sykes or F.S. was a famous World War II British commando knife.

These WWII veterans' accounts of combatives on the battlefield show why it's absolutely necessary to keep techniques simple and apply them explosively, brutally and with complete commitment.

While writing this book, I reconnected with Jim to ask him what he believed were the most important characteristics of combatives. Here's his list in his words:

1. **Simplicity.** It is absolutely essential to keep the mind uncluttered.
2. **Explosiveness.** Your mind-set should be "NO QUARTER!" Bewilder the opponent with the speed and intensity of the attack.
3. **Capability/Self-Awareness.** It is absolutely essential that you stay within your capabilities. This becomes very important as you age and the possible actions and techniques you can utilize decreases.
4. **Aggressiveness/Ferocity.** Think aggressively always. Never defend.
5. **Consequences.** Under no circumstance let your mind dwell on possible consequences.

HOW ARE COMBATIVES DIFFERENT FROM MARTIAL ARTS?

Combatives differ from martial arts in many ways. They are primarily made up of Western-based fighting skills but *may* also include techniques from or be influenced by Asian martial arts. There isn't a sport form of combatives. Unlike *taekwondo*, Brazilian *jiu-jutsu* or other well established martial arts, there is no universal governing body or rank structure. There is no *soki* (founder) or grandmaster. There *are* a growing number of combatives schools and burgeoning combatives organizations, but none have emerged as preeminent and are unlikely to.

Combatives are less well-known or understood than traditional martial arts. In my opinion, there are a number of reasons for this. Here are three:

1. **Combatives training hurts.** It's important the practitioner is confident that he or she can achieve street effectiveness. It's equally important he or she knows what street effectiveness feels like from firsthand experience. Contusions, lacerations and joint injuries are common. A lot of people just aren't willing to endure the intensity of proper combatives training.

2. **Combatives don't generate big revenues.** Children account for the majority of stereotypical martial arts school revenues. Children should NOT be taught combatives. This has limited the commercial proliferation of combatives schools, resulting in the public's general unawareness of it.

3. **Combatives training has a single purpose.** Combatives training doesn't provide the practitioner with any structure, discipline or other benefits derived from traditional martial arts. In the military, those things are provided by martial ethos. Combatives training only prepares you to defend yourself.

Combatives are not an art. Each year I design an irreverent T-shirt for our instructor staff and close associates. They're intentionally tongue in cheek. Some years back, the design I created to differentiate combatives from martial arts asked the question: "Wanna learn an art? Take up painting."

In martial arts training, the associated philosophical element and structure is desirable and beneficial for some. For others, achieving rank's the goal in which they can tangibly demonstrate long-term commitment to something with ever-increasing achievement. In a *Black Belt* interview with Executive Editor Robert W. Young, I explained the difference between combatives and martial arts focus this way, "It's a *jutsu* (skill) vs. a *do* (way [of life]) thing."

Recent commercialization has corrupted the purism of combatives focus on skill alone. It's likely the same thing happened as martial arts were commercialized. Today, it's not uncommon for people to complicate combatives with an idealistic framework, organizational hierarchy, institutional ranking and elongated curriculums—all in order to engage students over a longer period of time to increase revenues. In my opinion, these people are self-aggrandizers; they try to be "reality-based self-defense" messiahs. (Here's a hint: Check how many techniques or methods they name after themselves...) Look, combatives are finite. When they're made complicated, they're no longer combatives.

Lastly, martial artists generally tend to practice their system with reverence. Combatives practitioners tend to be irreverent. Many martial artists seem to be OK with bowing to a foreign flag and are capable of almost blind loyalty to their style or master. Students of combatives don't (and shouldn't) subordinate themselves—ever. They don't have "masters." Combatives practitioners train *with* their instructors not *under* them. Respect is earned by the instructor and not simply demanded of the student.

COMBATIVES THINKING

*J*eet kune do is perhaps the closest martial art to combatives because of the system's inherent flexibility, unrestrictive form and reductionist theory. Bruce Lee's well-documented development of JKD resulted in a gold mine of quotes that directly apply to combatives. Among the most applicable in regard to how I developed my combatives curriculum are the following:

Bruce Lee: *"It's not daily increase but decrease. Hack away the unessential."*
Combatives Corollary: I say, "Less is more." The more techniques you learn, the more difficult it is to maintain mastery of each. The more variations you have to choose from when attacked, the slower you respond. "Hick's Law" describes the time it takes for a person to make a decision as a function of the possible choices he or she has; this is called "choice reaction time." It should be obvious that reaction time increases exponentially with the number of response choices available. Combatives training results in significantly decreased reaction times.

Bruce Lee: *"I have not invented a 'new style,' composite, modified or otherwise that is set within distinct form as apart from 'this' method or 'that' method. On the contrary, I hope to free my followers from clinging to styles, patterns, or molds. ...Jeet Kune Do is not an organized institution that one can be a member of. Either you understand or you don't, and that is that."*
Combatives Corollary: Through the years, people have encouraged me to call my curriculum a "system" and name it after myself. I've never understood that because it's a compilation of techniques drawn from different sources. What I teach now isn't the same as what I taught years ago and won't be what I teach in the future. How could it be?

As threats emerge and adapt to countermeasures, as criminals develop their techniques, as life experience accumulates and as age interferes, I update my techniques, discarding some, incorporating new content or developing existing ones. The combatives sequences in my curriculum are designed by me. I suppose some of the individual techniques may be original as well, but look, it's *all* been done before. People have been attacking each other and defending themselves since the beginning of time. I'm not sure anyone can lay claim to an original thought when it comes to violence.

Many times founders become unable or unwilling to edit their courses, thoughts or techniques, especially when their name is attached to them. They're more prone to irrationally defend components of their systems even when another technique they were previously unaware of is proven equally effective or even superior. When that happens, their interest is no longer in providing the best solution to their students but in maintaining their own legacy, and *that's* plain bullshit.

Bruce Lee: *"Learn the principle, abide by the principle, and dissolve the principle. In short, enter a mold without being caged in it. Obey the principle without being bound by it."*

Combatives Corollary: One student of mine, who was a superior fighter in every respect, came to me when he started his own reality-based self-defense business. He hadn't trained with me for a couple of years. He wanted to know if he could start training with me again, saying he knew he'd benefit from my perspective on his development of techniques.

"Look, man," I said, "You're not a subordinate to me or anyone else. You're a peer. Go start your own training group and experiment with the techniques I beat into you. Continue your own personal development by working out efficiencies in how you apply the principles you learned from me. Don't be afraid of adding principles you develop yourself or abandoning ones I teach if they don't work for you anymore."

Bruce Lee: *"I believe the only way to teach anyone proper self-defense is to approach each individual personally. Each one of us is different and each one of us should be taught the correct form. By correct form I mean the most useful techniques the person is inclined toward. Find his ability and then develop these."*

Combatives Corollary: This stuff is pure gold! It's all about personal attributes. What my physique, coordination, speed, agility and mind-set allow me to do results in techniques I favor and rely on. It may simply be unrealistic for someone with significantly different attributes to effectively use the same techniques. I had a Mongo-strong student who could execute any technique in my curriculum. He trained with me on a weekly basis for six years, but trouble was by the third year, he still sucked as a fighter. He was slow. He never developed a rapid targeting thought process. He just wasn't effective.

Insisting on making him move and fight like me would have meant I failed as his instructor. Instead, I focused his training on ground and pound. We drilled on one- and two-leg takedowns. We drilled on suplex throws, leg drags and leg trips. I developed takedown transitions from the clinch for him. Once he got you on the ground, you were doomed. He was so strong and methodical that what worked best for him was to control his adversary, develop an advantage and then dominate him by pounding away.

Although I personally prefer to act so explosively, resolutely and powerfully that the fight is over before it can get grounded, I would've done this student a disservice by demanding the same from him. In my opinion, everyone should strive for balanced acumen in stand-up and ground fighting, but in this case, my guy achieved true personal proficiency by adopting a predominantly ground-oriented fighting style. He also had a concrete chin and could take punches that would've dropped me like I'd been shot. If he had to take a few licks to get your legs, it just meant you were going to pay that much more when he inevitably mounted you.

ARE COMBATIVES A STYLE?

I think it's wrong to characterize combatives as a "fighting style" because, as I've been quoted, "Martial arts are something you do *with* someone; combatives you do *to* someone."

The statement reflects my thinking that "fighting" is a protracted, reciprocal event.

In the sports of boxing and wrestling, both focus on reciprocal movements. For example, when one boxer punches, the other counterpunches. Both fighters are cognizant of how much time is left in the round, how many rounds are left in the fight and the presence of a referee. Similarly, when one wrestler shoots for his opponent's legs, the other sprawls and tries to convert the move to his advantage. Each wrestler is aware of the scoring ring boundary marked on the mat, how much time is left in the bout and the presence of the referee.

On the street, neither combatant considers a fight reciprocal. Still, when an attacker strikes, the intended victim has to initially defend himself. Combatives teaches that after defending against the first strike, you immediately, brutally and efficiently reverse the confrontational dynamic by attacking the attacker. The goal is to change from prey to predator so unexpectedly, so explosively and so violently that your attacker suddenly (and completely) understands *he's* the one at risk. *His* safety is in jeopardy. Predator becomes prey and, importantly, behaves like it.

You can't afford to give your attacker a second chance because on the street there are:

- no time limits
- no weight classes
- no rules
- no fouls
- no referee

There is only consequence—for the both of you.

When I was first learning about fighting, my dad explained how to explosively reverse roles with your attacker this way. "You always start fighting like you mean to kill a guy," he'd say.

I love my Dad, but at 12 years old, I used to think, "Man, I'm just fighting over lunch money and girls. Dad's a little weird."

It wasn't until later in life I realized what an essential premise of street fighting that mind-set is. His point was you have to *immediately* eclipse your attacker's level of violence with your own. You can always choose to back off—not kick someone in the face when they're down or hit him in the throat—but you may *not* be able to catch up to his rapidly escalating level of violence before you're hurt too badly and consequently can't.

Your initial response has to make your attacker *doubt*, has to make him *fear*, has to fill him with *dread* and make him *regret* he chose to attack you. Defending, by its very nature, is losing. You've got to continuously attack to win. Huh, turns out my old man's not such a weirdo.

ELEMENTS OF COMBATIVES CURRICULUM

Developing an effective combatives curriculum is a continual process of asking yourself, "What can I get rid of?" and not saying, "I should add that just in case." A combatives curriculum must be kept free of corrupting influences and strictly include just what's essential for self-defense. Resist the nagging urge to include a "nice to have," a "just in case," or the dreaded "another tool in the toolbox" technique.

Don't get me wrong. I'm not suggesting curriculum developers shouldn't look at new techniques, consider different styles, read about innovations or review their curriculum's utility. What I'm saying is in order for a curriculum to remain characteristically combative it has to be:

- lean
- valid
- relevant
- practical

As I said previously, I believe in Hick's Law, which asserts choice reaction time increases with the number of alternatives available. In other words, if you know three different techniques for the same type of attack, you'll react more slowly than if you knew only one. Choice reaction time also increases under duress.

That's why in combatives, we intentionally limit the curriculum, include only the most easily learned and effective techniques, develop a student's combative mind-set and instill combative principles that can be applied universally to many situations.

My own combatives curriculum is an eclectic mix of WWII hand-to-hand combat and Philippine martial arts-influenced, empty-hand and weapons techniques (stick and knife). It also includes old school *jujutsu*, elements of *muay* Thai, "jailhouse rock[3]," barroom brawling and back-alley "catch-as-catch-can" kick ass.

When I first put my curriculum together in the early '80s, I didn't care where the techniques came from and I still don't because it's all about effectiveness. If someone demonstrates something tomorrow that rocks my world, I'll dump the corresponding technique in my curriculum the minute it's validated. To me, a technique is "validated" if people of different skill levels can master it adequately in a reasonable amount of time and execute it under duress in various adverse environmental conditions.

Each year, I conduct a courseware curriculum review. My instructors and I discuss each technique's continuing relevance to our clients' operational reality and our ever-changing student population's ability to understand, learn and master the technique. We also discuss how it's held up under duress by reviewing any after-action reports of its use on deployment.

The most important consideration of any individual combatives technique is whether it will work in real-world conditions. Determining whether it will or won't isn't easy. A technique may work with a compliant *uke* (training partner). It may also work with a "pillar" assault—a demonstration technique in which a training partner attacks his opponent in a way that supports the technique used to counter it. A technique may also work in perfect environmental conditions, like a well-lit area with sure footing and physical parity of combatants, but it may fail under actual conditions when performed under duress. That's why the question I ask regarding each technique is this: "Will it work if a person is attacked unexpectedly, in disadvantageous conditions and by a committed assailant?" If the answer is no or if it takes the rest of your life to make it work, it's probably not worth the effort.

By the way, just because a technique is included in a black-and-white book (circa 1940s) written by any number of combatives "forefathers" doesn't confirm it was used in battle, resulted in the death of an enemy combatant or that it was ever successfully used in a self-defense situation. Some of the old self-defense and combatives techniques represented in those books (and believe me when I say I've read most of them) suck. Heresy? If you think so, you haven't objectively scrutinized them or tried using them against active, animated aggressors in training.

---

[3] Jailhouse Rock is an actual informal fighting style that prisoners taught each other in U.S. penitentiaries in the 1950s and 1960s.

CURRENT STATE OF COMBATIVES

Combatives schools, groups, Web sites and blogs are proliferating. What could loosely be called a combatives "community" (in the absolute broadest sense of the term) has emerged. Within that loose community, there are instructors and practitioners who faithfully adhere to WWII combatives techniques and those who don't. There are also instructors and practitioners of martial arts who've successfully boiled their respective styles down to the absolute essentials, making them "combatives-like" hybrids.

Amidst endless Internet-forum arguments—from the infinite and irritating "my combatives are better than your combatives" or the equally annoying "my instructor is better than your instructor"—*some* combatives common ground has surfaced:

- the desire to practice a simple, efficient, effective and powerful form of self-defense
- an agreement of how important total mental aggression and commitment are to successful physical application
- an acceptance of the use of hyperviolence to immediately stop an attack
- the abrupt and explosive application of all individual techniques
- the use of pre-emptive tactics when avoidance is impossible

Combatives are usually practiced in unorthodox and innocuous places like basements, warehouses or after hours in gymnasiums by people who want succinct, extreme self-defense. Training focuses on developing individual combatives skill based on personal attributes. It also fosters a combatives mind-set, which enables students to prevail in self-defense situations.

If you're unaware of or can't access a grass-roots combatives group, you may have to sort through the modern combatives landscape in order to seek quality training from a commercial school. That can be challenging because one result of the proliferation of civilian schools is vastly conflicting ideas and approaches to combatives training. Confirm the instructor's credentials and that the curriculum taught can be effectively used by you for self-defense before you commit to training.

READER BEWARE!

As you approach your training, be wary of "combatives commandos"—absolutists and shameless self-promoters or "cult of personality" types who make sweeping, unsubstantiated statements concerning their proprietary system or techniques and, for that matter, their personal abilities, backgrounds and experience.

No one should exalt themselves at the expense of others by bad-mouthing any school other than their own. The bottom line is when pride eclipses reality and turns malicious, this ridiculous posturing gets truly detestable. When any instructor can't see at least some merit in other styles or dismisses all alternative techniques while loudly professing his way is the *only* way, you should run away.

Internet forums provide an anonymous haven for the obnoxious. Online, they're able to make unequivocal statements about techniques or systems and state heavily opinionated judgments regarding the efficacy of a style as fact. Forum posts that indicate an unwillingness to consider valid alternative techniques reveal quite a lot about who's at the keyboard. Remember that before you find yourself wrestling a pig because "you both get dirty and the pig likes it."

The guy manning the keyboard on the other end of that smarm is more than likely the lightweight wearing Coke-bottle lenses who's *never* been in a fight but can quote chapter and verse of any self-defense reference and routinely bullies any forum member daring to dissent his opinions. Generically, you know who I'm talking about; his posts are laced with insinuation suggesting he has some kind of "special" knowledge or experience. He's condescending, basks in the adulation of junior forum members and decisively flames anyone who disagrees with him. Yeah—that one. What an asshole.

There's no way to empirically validate ludicrous claims made on the Internet; it's insane to try. Here's the thing: Somewhere, there will always be someone who's absolutely convinced "combat" *tai chi* (or whatever) is the Rosetta stone of whippin' ass. It doesn't matter—perhaps universally—that his belief could be disputed and proven incorrect. To that guy, combat tai chi is the heat.

It doesn't matter why he believes it, he just does. He may have a whole horde of students who revere him and embrace combat tai chi, wear black special-ops-killer tai chi pajamas, tattoo secret symbols on their bodies and assault the Internet forums en masse to flame all non-believers. They may award ranks from spud belt to grand pooh-bah. So what? Chastising them is a waste of breath. Trying to convince the combat tai chi zealots their techniques are harmless won't have any impact on them. In fact the more their beliefs are assailed, the more likely they'll vigorously defend them—sometimes to the point of obduracy. Who fucking cares?

In over 25 years of teaching combatives, I'm surer today of what I don't know than what I do. There's too much information about fighting available, too many useful techniques, too many tough guys around, too many variations of style and approach to combatives for anyone to claim they're the burning bush; enough already with the self-licking ice cream cones and brainwashing. Look for an instructor who encourages their students to be curious, do their own research and remain open-minded. Get away from the computer, get off your ass and BANG!

CHAPTER 2
REALITIES OF A CONFRONTATION

Street violence is wildly unpredictable. It happens lightning fast, usually when conditions are most advantageous to the attacker and least advantageous to the victim, like when the victim is noticeably preoccupied. Use of weapons is prevalent in street crime, and even though there's statistically less crime today than in the past, the use of violence has dramatically increased.

Criminal predilection for using violence and weapons should alarm you. After all, thugs aren't necessarily skilled with the weapons they use. They don't regulate their use of force or adhere to a use-of-force continuum. A criminal doesn't know how to hit you "just hard enough" with a pipe to only knock you out. He may kill you whether he meant to or not. Unskilled use of weapons has resulted in unintended murders. Criminals and thugs commonly justify themselves by saying things like:

- "I didn't mean to kill her."
- "I was just trying to scare them."
- "The gun just went off."
- "He wouldn't stop fighting back so I kept stabbing him."

Add an element of intoxication, drug-induced fury, racial motivation, sexually-urgent rage or any other of a hundred variables, and you've got a toxic formula for serious injury or death.

Then there's the ungovernable element of chance to consider.

Superior fighters can lose; in fact, they *do* lose. That's what makes competitive fighting like mixed martial arts so enthralling. There's always the chance of a huge upset. That's exciting in the ring where the consequence of an unexpected knockout is loss of pride, prize money or a championship. It's less exciting on the street when an unexpected KO could result in a vegetative state, paralysis or death.

Most people don't develop a personal relationship with violence because criminal violence is intimidating and repugnant. Instead, they formulate their understanding and general perception of street violence from television and cinematic dramatizations and personal anecdotes—sometimes accurate but more often inaccurate—rather than firsthand experience.

Dramatizations intentionally elongate violent attacks in order to heighten suspense and increase audience impact. The result is the audience draws the incorrect conclusion that there's a lot of time to see a street attack developing and plenty of time to take action to avoid it.

Here's an example of how this skewed perception is portrayed in combat-action movies. A Soviet rocket-propelled grenade or RPG-7 travels at a rate of 965 feet per second. In combat movies (for the sake of drama), the rockets "rocket" so slowly the audience can see them flying toward the target. Laughably, actors not only "see" the projectile but also have time to yell, "Incoming!" before bracing for impact.

Nothing could be further from the truth. One of the terrifying things about an RPG is its immediacy. In reality you're not going to leap out of the way. If you're the target, you're unlikely to see any firing signature before impact. There's no time to react, you're just blown up. The same inaccurate portrayal of time is true even in more typical, everyday dramatizations like a carjacking that takes three minutes. A real carjacking? That takes about five seconds.

PRACTICING AVOIDANCE

On the street, criminals have to get close to victimize you. They know they can't reveal their intention too early or potential victims would vanish. A weapon has to be ready to use as the criminal moves toward a victim, but still kept concealed. Criminals are apprehensive. They don't want to be seen by eyewitnesses or be caught. These things manifest in demeanor and movement that can be identified once you know what to look for and once you develop sound situational awareness.

It's even true in the case of an RPG-7. On the battlefield, a situationally-aware soldier looks for anomalous movements at or around tactically-sound firing positions. He scans for furtive actions made by people who know they're going to be shot dead if they're seen shouldering and aiming an RPG. That kind of apprehension and fear results in erratic movement. Soldiers are more watchful at choke points where it would make sense for any weapon to be deployed against them. Situational awareness doesn't negate the possibility of attack, but it does lessen the potential for being surprised.

The application of situational awareness is universal. Whether it's in a hostile, war-torn country or here in the United States, look for the same kinds of behaviors around the types of choke points found wherever you are. For example, in a permissive environment, an ATM continually presents targets of opportunity—people with cash—for criminals. You should have a heightened sense of situational awareness around ATMs because, in effect, they're choke points and criminals will exhibit similar behaviors due to *their* apprehension.

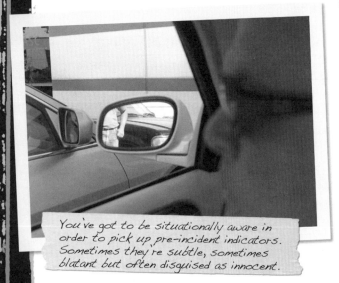

You've got to be situationally aware in order to pick up pre-incident indicators. Sometimes they're subtle, sometimes blatant but often disguised as innocent.

An insurgent is going to seek a tactically sound firing position for the deployment of his RPG-7. A criminal is going to seek a tactically sound position for himself to rob you at an ATM. A soldier scans for furtive movement in Baghdad, and you scan for furtive movements in Baton Rouge. Both of you have a heightened sense of situational awareness around the types of choke points common in your respective environments.

Victims often say things like, "I didn't see him before he hit me." Actually, it'd be more accurate to say, "I didn't *notice* him." Criminals (or any attacker) physically occupy space before they attack. They have to see their victims so they're usually in the victim's line of sight. They're just not *noticed* by their victims who are preoccupied, disinterested or disinclined to believe any violent crime could possibly happen to them.

In the months following 9/11, Tom Ridge, the newly appointed Director of Homeland Security, frequently said, "Americans have to be vigilant and stay watchful." But he never said what to be watchful for or what specifically there was to be vigilant about.

What he meant was Americans had to be increasingly aware of targeting behaviors. In other words, what it looks like when a terrorist or criminal is conducting preoperational surveillance, what a "probe" (a nonintrusive test undertaken to gauge the awareness, alertness and potential responses of victims) looks like, and what the bad guys *appear* to be doing just before they strike.

SITUATIONAL AWARENESS, PRE-INCIDENT INDICATORS AND ATTACK-RECOGNITION SKILLS

Situational awareness has become a buzzword used in regard to both personal security and military operations. It's frequently used under the assumption that everyone knows *specifically* what it means even when most civilians don't. So here is my definition:

"Situational awareness" is a cumulative alertness to threat and your environment. It enables you to notice pre-incident indicators, which are odd movements or anomalies given the situation. Cumulatively, pre-incident indicators create a visual unlikely circumstance consistent with either a contrived situation or predatorial behavior.

"Attack-recognition skill" is your aptitude in comprehending pre-incident indicators relative to evolving or imminent attacks. You can't recognize a potential attack without having the situational awareness to notice and make sense of subtle pre-incident indicators.

Don't misunderstand, having well-developed attack-recognition skills doesn't mean you're paranoid and prone to overreacting to any stimulus or looking for bad guys around every corner. Good attack-recognition skills become second nature, helping you discern when an attack may be imminent. Any one pre-incident indicator is likely nothing. If you notice *two*, pay close attention. When three or more pre-incident indicators are present, you're probably in an emerging threat situation that deserves your *complete* attention and, very likely, some type of action.

Here are some universal pre-incident indicators of imminent street crime or pending violent assault:

No Cover for Action, No Cover for Status

Jack

Me

This is tradecraft speak for anyone who doesn't appear to have a reason for being in a particular place and doing what they appear to be doing. In this picture, Jack doesn't appear to have a reason for hanging out, remaining stationary or just looking around. He's in a parking lot without anything in his hands. He doesn't have car keys jangling in his hand like he's getting ready to either lock/unlock his own car. He's not walking purposefully. His head's on a swivel, potentially looking around for eyewitnesses, police, security or his escape route before he attacks.

He's also tentatively touching the hem of his T-shirt. When criminals are in motion and about to attack but haven't gotten their weapon in their hand yet, they have a tendency to touch the weapon for reassurance or to dink with their cover garment—T-shirt, hoody, or jacket—in preparation for the draw.

If both hands are in a central pocket of a hoody or if one hand is in a windbreaker pocket, look for the "printing" that occurs as the edges of a weapon press up against the cover garment material.

Sudden Change in Someone's Status

My hands are tied up as I open my door when Jack's status suddenly changes. He was just loitering, but now he's closing in on me and his focus is clearly on me. Nothing else has changed. If I was situationally aware, I'd have noticed his change of status and movement toward me. But I'm not situationally aware and didn't notice. Consequently Jack's obviously decided I'm preoccupied and unaware of him.

Correlation of Movement

In this example, I'd have to deduce Jack's not likely to offer his help to put my bags in the trunk, so why's he following so closely behind me? And what's up with how he's looking around? If I was situationally aware, I'd be suspicious of his intent and might suddenly turn abruptly in his direction, look at my watch while staying aware of his reaction, then hurry away in a safe direction as if I'd forgotten something.

It's just a ruse to gauge his reaction. If Jack were to slow down or "stutter step⁴" and then aimlessly wander around, not really getting closer to me or moving away, I'd have good reason to believe he was "holding off" his victim. He's still considering me for target value but is also seeing what other developments might occur before fully committing to the attack. The bottom line? If I start hurrying away using my ploy and he correlates with my movement…Ruh roh.

Hidden Hands That Cause Unnatural Movement

I haven't alerted on Jack because I've got my nose in my BlackBerry—what a dope! I missed his lifted elbow, indicating he's retrieving something. Even if I didn't see a weapon, the fact his path is deliberately intersecting mine and he's put something into his hand would be enough for me to alert on him. All these subtle behaviors are just more pieces of the pre-incident indicator, attack-recognition puzzle.

People walking normally swing both their hands naturally, unless they're occupied like when they carry something. Conversely, when anyone traps a hand under an armpit or hides one behind a leg while they're walking, it may indicate an effort to conceal a weapon.

The way to develop acute sensitivity to pre-incident indicators is to develop a predator's mind-set. If *you* were seeking a positional advantage, where would you stand? If *you* were getting ready to sucker someone, what would you do? Look for those behaviors.

Here's another example of how all these subtle pre-indicators combine:

When I first started my business in the early 1990s, I opened a combatives training facility in a rundown section of town. It was located in a row of commercial bays that were leased to a variety of auto-industry businesses.

After shutting down one night around 10, I pulled into an adjacent all-night drugstore a block away to replenish the facility's first-aid kit. The parking lot was empty but well lit. I parked near the entrance and went inside. I was carrying my Glock 27, a compact .40-caliber pistol. I had it well concealed beneath a sweatshirt in what we call "the felony carry"—in front, inside the waistband and on the strong side.

After collecting all the stuff I needed, I walked up to the counter to pay. While the clerk rang me up, three 20-something kids came inside, inappropriately loud and overly animated. They queued up behind me. As I pulled cash out of my pocket to pay, one of the kids leaned forward. He reached past me—as if to grab some gum or mints—turned his head, looked directly at my cash and retracted his hand without picking anything up. He stepped back.

I remember saying to myself, "If these knuckleheads exit behind me before they could've bought anything…. I've got a problem." I took my change from the clerk, grabbed the bag in my weak-side hand and left. Sure enough within seconds, I heard the door open and footsteps behind me. I threw a glance over my shoulder and the three guys were behind me, walking in my direction. They weren't talking or joking anymore.

Yeah, you always get a little adrenal rush when you see it coming.

So now what? The threat's proximity to you, whether the threat's armed or could be armed and whether or not avenues of escape are accessible to you, will determine your next action—and there are almost infinite variations.

FOUR SOLUTIONS—ONE ATTACK

Here's a matrix that articulates some of those infinite variations and how simple or complicated threats and responses can be. I'm going to describe one evolving threat scenario and provide four completely correct but different solutions based on time and distance as they relate to the threat's proximity to you and the increasing potential for violent escalation.

---

[4] A stutter step is a sudden break in the rhythm of someone's gait, an unnatural pause or erratic movement.

The Threat at 20 Yards

As you leave the mall, your BlackBerry vibrates; it's an e-mail you've been waiting for. Despite wanting to open and read it, you're being watchful and notice a guy near your vehicle. He's standing in the parking lot, doesn't have keys in his hand and has no bags with him. He's alone. He's loitering and one of his hands is low and behind his thigh. You think that's odd.

Your Solution at 20 Yards

You draw your pistol and shoot him. KIDDING!!!! Seriously, the fact you noticed him acting strangely and can't see a hand is reason enough to be suspicious of his intent. You choose to *AVOID* the situation altogether and either:

1. Take a circuitous route to your vehicle.

2. Stop where you are and give the situation a chance to dissipate.

3. Go back inside the mall and wait the weirdo out.

The Threat at Three Yards

Let's say you couldn't resist the urge to open that e-mail. Because you're reading it, you don't notice the guy near your car. You're startled when he suddenly intercepts you, stepping into your path and blocking your forward motion.

Your Solution at Three Yards

PRE-EMPT an attack by disrupting the potential threat, preventing the situation from developing into something worse than it is. That doesn't necessarily mean you should take combative action—unless your assessment indicates you should. Your pre-emptive actions could be to:

1. Verbally warn the person to "BACK OFF!".

2. Get your hands up in front of you and back away or bolt.

3. Brandish a nonlethal weapon (pepper spray) and verbally warn the threat while backing away.

The Threat Becomes an Attack/ a Weapon Appears

The thug pulls his weapon, menacing you with it. He demands your wallet. This is surreal. It's so foreign an experience to you that you're still trying to get your head around what's really happening.

Your Solution When a Weapon Appears

COMPLY (or appear to comply). Nothing you own is worth dying over. Nothing. You can always get more stuff, but you can't get another life. You're at a tactical disadvantage, haven't been seen by anyone who might intervene and are facing serious injury or death if this dude makes good on his threat to kill you if you don't, "HAND OVER YOUR SHIT RIGHT NOW!" You should:

1. Hand over your shit…ah, right now.

2. Get one hand as close to the weapon as you can in order to clear your body of the weapon's line of attack and visualize your next move.

3. Keep talking, not yelling—you've got to de-escalate the situation. Try to chill this cretin out to keep it from going south.

The Situation Goes South

You hand over your valuables but have a sinking feeling in your gut. In the ensuing pregnant pause, he checks left and right and you just *know* he's going to use that weapon…

Your Solution When the Situation Goes South

FIGHT! Here it is. The terrible delta. Your point of no return. The second you believe you're going to be injured or killed, whether you're prepared to or not, whether you know how to fight or not, you're faced with only two outcomes:

1. He gets to do what he's going to (injure or kill you).

2. You get to keep him from doing it.

When your reality is the last example, there isn't another resolution. You can't talk a vicious dog out of biting you once it's decided to bite. The reality of the situation has eclipsed reason. Bullets are too fast and knives cut too quickly to let the situation go any further. You have to get control over the situation by attacking in self-defense. You see? This is the reason you've got to be situationally aware for pre-incident indicators and use your attack-recognition skills. You want to act as early as possible to avoid violent street confrontations.

In the second section of this book, I'll describe the corresponding physical actions you should take and why. Hopefully, at this point in the book, I've articulated the unpredictable, unstable realities of street violence well enough for you to feel compelled to reconsider what you may have previously thought you knew about the dynamics of violent crime.

JUNGLE RULES AND THE NATURE OF PEOPLE

There are no completely reliable outcomes when you use violence in self-defense. Need an example? Shoot one guy, he falls over dead. Shoot another guy with the same caliber weapon in the same part of his body, and he doesn't realize he's been shot and continues to attack you. Shoot still a third, and he stops, grabs the wound, drops to his knees and screams. What's up with that?

Here's another: You smack a guy square in the face and knock him out. You smack another guy (same size as the first) square in the face and he stumbles backward, wrinkles his brow then charges at you, now *truly* pissed off. You smack a third guy (right, same size) square in the face, and he stumbles backward—holding a hand out in your direction signaling he's had enough—spits Chiclets and puts his hand over his bleeding pie hole.

When it comes to violence, there are very, very few constants, and that reality is just too unsettling for most people to deal with. They want unqualified, definitive answers, but there are none. Here are the only ground truths I know of concerning people and their quest for certainty in dealing with street violence:

People generally want no-exception techniques ("So if an attacker does this, and I do that, I'll definitely be OK...right?")

Wrong. Fighting on the street is anything but an "if a then b, if b then c" algorithm. The trouble with trying to develop, identify or implement no-exception techniques is there aren't any. Too many variables affect any attack's outcome for there to be a consistently reliable, formulaic solution to an attack. The results you get using any technique are always conditional.

Most people don't think about being victimized.

Every single day someone gets raped, someone is robbed, someone suffers an assault and someone ends up dead as a result of violence. Not one of those unfortunate souls woke up that day really believing it could happen to them—maybe a neighbor, a relative or even a friend but definitely not themselves.

People want assurance, reassurance or validation that their "style" of self-defense will guarantee success in all situations.

There are no guarantees in violence no matter what you know or think you know. You can train like an animal, be uberfit, tactically brilliant, phenomenally skilled with weapons and walk around in a state of situational-awareness clarity approaching crystal and still be killed by a half-stoned, unskilled crackhead. It happens.

People want to be sure they're about to be attacked before they take any action to defend themselves.

You can't know the unknowable. I'm often quoted saying, "Final confirmation of any attack is the attack." You can't afford that kind of confirmation. You can't divine criminal intent. The truth is even the criminal doesn't know where or how the attack will end most of the time.

Don't believe it?

A guy robs a woman at an ATM. There aren't any witnesses and no one's intervening, so he decides to rape his victim. He pulls her into an alley. She starts to fight and scream. He strangles her in order to shut her up.

A young thug holds up a couple outside their hotel while they walk to their car. The male victim responds a little too quickly and reaches for his wallet. The thug—whose dumbass finger is on the trigger of his pistol—gets startled and yanks the trigger, shooting the male. The woman starts to scream. The kid doesn't want any witnesses so he shoots her too.

When you're attacked, the only thing you can be certain of is the presence of uncertainty. Taking avoidant action as early as possible at the first indication there may be a problem is the best course of action. Wait any longer and you may be screwed.

People generally want to know they won't get into trouble for doing what they know they need to do in order to pre-empt an imminent attack.

But self-defense situations are conundrums. Assurances are impossible. The fact is you may have to hit someone first to avoid serious injury or death. I'm pretty sure it's illegal to do that in any state, despite the thousands of situations you can conjure up proving you might suffer severe injury or death otherwise.

So if the law says you can't hit someone first to avoid being hurt or killed, then you need to get hit first? Wow. Not a great concept. What if you're knocked out? Maybe it's not a fist your attacker just hit you with in the gut, maybe he had a knife in his fist. Round and round it goes.

Here's an exemplifying excerpt from a story in the March 2004 issue of *Esquire* that journalist Tucker Carlson of CNN's *Crossfire* and MSNBC's *Tucker!* wrote when I took him to Iraq:

"Less than an hour into the drive (from Safwan, Kuwait to Baghdad), we got the first sign that someone was watching us. One of the Citroëns in our convoy radioed to say that a pickup truck was coming up from behind extremely fast, even faster than we were going. Jack Altizer [in the follow car] had already picked up transmissions on his surveillance gear indicating that two people nearby were communicating on walkie-talkies. It looked like the classic setup to a carjacking: spotter by the side of the road sees Westerners in a convoy; gunmen in a chase vehicle pull up alongside and force them off the road. Or just shoot them.

I was riding in one of the SUVs, a mud-splattered Nissan, in the backseat behind Kelly and Bill Frost, another former Marine. Kelly and I were talking about the approaching pickup when suddenly it appeared right next to us.

There were three young Arab men inside. They were inches away from our driver's-side window, maintaining our speed and giving us hard looks. Kelly's voice never changed its tone. He raised his MP5 off his lap, extended it across Bill's chest, and pointed the muzzle at the men in the pickup. They hit the brakes hard, disappearing into our rearview mirror. Bill never took his eyes off the road. Kelly kept up the conversation as though nothing had happened."

Courtesy of Tucker Carlson and *Esquire*

In Baghdad, Tucker Carlson stands in front of the Hands of Victory monument, which celebrates the end of the Iran-Iraq War.

Photo courtesy of Kelly McCann

People not experienced with the threat of violence or actual violence might say (with considerable smarm), "Well! Aggressive behavior begets aggressive behavior. Brandishing a weapon is over the top!"

But see, here's the math:

The men in the truck were suspicious because of their age and their grooming; they looked like Fedayeen. Their correlation with us at speeds in excess of 100 mph was odd enough and these guys were attempting to pass us! Funny how they suddenly appeared just after we intercepted radio transmissions that indicated we were passing by—that would be correlation wouldn't it? At least THREE pre-incident indicators were present in the situation that day and that was enough because...

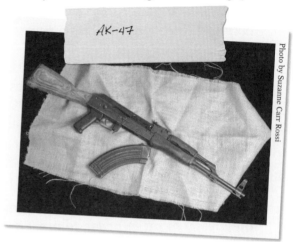

AK-47

Photo by Suzanne Carr Rossi

...an AK-47 fires a projectile at around 2,300 feet per second. If I hadn't brandished my weapon to demonstrate a willingness to kill them if they behaved badly and instead one of them simply lifted an AK muzzle above the car's window line and fired, there would've been no way to avoid being shot. Would they have hit Bill? Me? Tucker? Or just our vehicle? Worse, maybe all of us? I don't know, but they'd have certainly hit something. We simply couldn't afford to find out. By pre-empting their attack, we avoided the whole thing.

It would've been inappropriate to actually fire on them without one last furtive movement or some other missing piece of the emerging-attack puzzle. I let the events develop as long as I was willing to. What's most important about the incident is that pre-emptive action kept an imminent attack from happening. You don't have to like the way violence works, but that doesn't change the way it does.

Oh yeah, what happened outside the drug store...

I turned around gripping but not drawing my pistol and said, "Don't." The three guys stopped dead, obviously having seen my movement to clear my cover garment and that I had gripped what must obviously be a pistol. They didn't need to see anything else. They just said, "No problem, man. No problem. Be cool," and turned in the opposite direction. Had I been wrong in my assessment, I imagine they would've been a helluva lot more surprised and vocal—"Whoa man! What're you *doing*?" The fact is they knew what they were going to do and suddenly realized I knew what they were going to do. That meant they couldn't capitalize on surprise as an advantage. I've no doubt they intended to kick me to the curb and rob or carjack me. It got too hard. It was just business to them, besides, if not me then someone else.

Your decision to use violence has consequences. Your decision to not use it does, too. It's a Morton's Fork dilemma—two equally unpleasant alternatives.

PHYSIOLOGICAL EFFECTS OF IMMINENT DANGER

Perhaps the most important tenet inculcated throughout my combatives curriculum is that everyone is vulnerable to the physiological effects of imminent danger. If you aren't situationally aware for pre-incident indicators, it's highly likely any attack will initially startle you. The onset of the physiological effects of imminent danger is normally triggered by a startle stimulus. They potentially become disabling. The effects worsen in severity as you realize you're in a personally dangerous situation and understand the gravity of its consequences.

The physiological effects of imminent danger cause what I call "duress dysfunctions" that diminish a person's normal ability to perform tasks. The more complex a task is and the more extensively minor motor movements are involved, the more severely you're diminished trying to do it.

The only way to completely negate the physiological effects of imminent danger is through what's

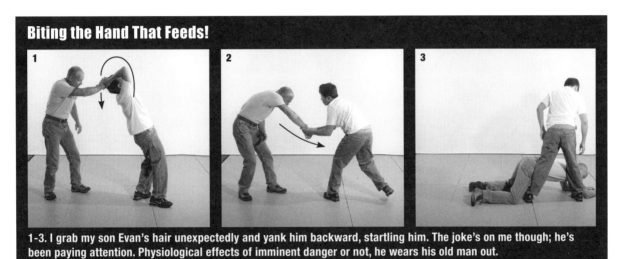

Biting the Hand That Feeds!

1-3. I grab my son Evan's hair unexpectedly and yank him backward, startling him. The joke's on me though; he's been paying attention. Physiological effects of imminent danger or not, he wears his old man out.

called "frequency of experience." In other words, you'd have to confront life-threatening situations so frequently they become your norm as opposed to the aberration. If that were the case, as they say, "You might not survive the cure."

What are some of the physiological effects of imminent danger?

Let's start with **diminished fine motor skills**. Fine-motor manipulation becomes extremely difficult, if not impossible, when you've been startled and are under duress. Unfortunately, a lot of common self-defense techniques require fine-motor manipulation because they're developed without regard for duress dysfunctions.

For example, consider a simple finger lock, like the "small circle *jujitsu*," with a really small axis of rotation. It's hilarious to do in a dojo or training environment because it slams people to the ground really quickly. You can lay someone out and literally wipe the mat with them. The problem with techniques like this for street use is that you've got to catch that finger when both you and the attacker are amped and he's shaking it in your face. Your second problem is he's balling his other hand into a fist to punch the shit out of you.

On the street, your attacker is fully animated and will retract whatever he throws out at you as quickly as he put it there. In most martial arts demonstrations, the attacking arm and fist are left extended so the self-defense technique can be executed.

Students are deluded into thinking these kinds of techniques are streetworthy based on how fast they can apply them in a dojo under training conditions and how effective they are on someone who leaves their arm there for the taking. Sorry, but I cry, "Bullshit!"

Keep your techniques combatively simple. Minimize any chance of a "miss." Incorporate as few movements as necessary and rely on powerful, gross motor skills. For example:

The KISS Principle (Keep It Simple, Sir)

1. Based on the look on Jack's face, a simple spike kick to his sac worked pretty well. It's lightning fast, comes from below his line of vision, doesn't telegraph at all, is pretty hard to miss with and is a gross-motor movement.

2. Or this straight knee to the groin.

3. Or this quick vault out of line and groin strike.

The next physiological effect of imminent danger we'll look at is **auditory exclusion**. When you've been startled by a sudden life-threatening situation, a phenomenon largely attributed to the brain's cortex occurs. The cortex "prioritizes" incoming stimuli, blocking some and letting through others. There's evidence to suggest the cause of auditory exclusion may be partially attributed to the rapid increase in blood pressure when someone's hyperstimulated by startle.

The sudden spike in blood pressure interferes with cochlear blood flow, which is a function of "cochlear perfusion pressure" or the delicate balance between mean-arterial pressure and inner-ear fluid. People who've experienced this report that they hear rushing, roaring or ringing sounds.

Think about it. If you go to the range and shoot one round without hearing protection, your ears ring for awhile. In combat, you don't wear hearing protection. Yet after having been ambushed, despite all the gunfire and other noise, you can hear just freakin' fine once you're clear of the danger.

Another effect is **tunnel vision**. This phenomenon is caused by the sudden flood of oxygen and adrenaline into the bloodstream from startle and rage. Peripheral vision is eliminated. It's like looking though a paper towel tube or as if you rubbed both your eyes really hard with your fists then suddenly opened them. What was your peripheral vision now appears dazzling and full of tiny, super bright dots.

Another effect is a **mental fugue state**. A fugue state can result from cognitive dissonance or confusion. This happens when you hold two conflicting thoughts in the mind simultaneously. In other words, your brain is yelling, "RUN" and "HIT HIM " at the same time.

Fugue severity is worsened by the importance of the conflicting thoughts, especially when they relate to self-image. For example, your self-image is one of strength and courage, but you're scared and know that people may notice you're scared.

One Attack and Three Effects

1. Jack yokes me up unexpectedly on the street. I see him fumbling with his shirt and I think, "GUN!!" I suddenly realize how serious the situation is.

2. Because of the sudden adrenaline rush, only the center of my vision is clear. I've also got roaring in my ears.

3. Somehow I foul his draw, throwing a hand down, trapping his hand against his body and loading my elbow. I can't see anything except his hand trying to pull the gun.

4. Keeping forward pressure against him, I unload my elbow and try to put his head into the next county.

The last three effects we'll discuss here are tremor, palpitation and visual slowdown.

Tremor is when uncontrollable, unintentional but somewhat rhythmic oscillations occur to one or more of your body parts. For example, your hands shaking due to fear, anxiety, panic and/or rage. The detrimental effect of tremor should be obvious. If you're trying to use a technique that requires precision or deft hand placement, you're in trouble.

Palpitation is one of the most disconcerting physiological effects of imminent danger because there is no way to quickly calm a racing heart. When you're startled, your heart will hammer in your chest. It's not uncommon for a person's heartbeat to race 200 to 300 beats per minute when stressed. Studies have proven

"GUN!!!"

Jack rips open the door of my car, and leading with his pistol, he gets in. My heart feels like it's going to explode out of my chest.

physical tasks that require precision are exponentially harder to achieve above 175 beats per minute; fine-motor techniques will fail you. Because combatives are practiced as a gross application of force—they're not precise—they alleviate major skill degradation.

Visual slowdown is layman terminology for a condition known as "tachypsychia." This phenomenon is believed to be caused by abnormally high levels of dopamine and epinephrine being instantaneously introduced into the bloodstream during events of extreme duress. The symptom is an erratic perception of time. Events are usually perceived in slow motion but objects may also be perceived with "trails" as if blurred by speed.

The gravity of my situation hits when Jack thrusts his pistol toward me. Everything seems to move in slow motion yet my heart and brain are racing.

There are many other physical manifestations of fear and panic that occur when you're under duress including voice "quavering," difficulty swallowing and dry mouth. Unfortunately, these are also observable cues to predators indicating you're frightened.

HOW TO MITIGATE DURESS DYSFUNCTIONS

You're headed for a colossal failure—when the consequences couldn't be greater—if the system or techniques you've grown to trust are based on either an inaccurate appraisal of what your abilities will actually be when you're attacked or an inaccurate understanding of how street violence actually occurs.

Combatives are designed to mitigate duress dysfunctions by requiring far less precision than other forms of self-defense. Combatives techniques adhere to Hick's Law by limiting choices and ensuring those choices are techniques that can be reliably executed despite performance dysfunctions. This subsequently improves reaction time and your effectiveness, maximizing your chances of success in unexpected street violence.

I also wanted to mention this: There are a tremendous number of trainers who believe you can accumulate enough repetitions of a task through training (for example, using a reverse wrist manipulation for a lapel grab attack) that, even when startled and under severe life-threatening duress, your skill will not be diminished. They also believe that having achieved a great number of repetitions, you'll be able to accomplish the task without conscious thought. They refer to this level of performance as having built the task into your "muscle memory."

The problem is muscle memory doesn't exist; muscles can't remember anything. I interviewed an ergonomic engineer when I updated my curriculum in the mid-1980s and asked him about muscle memory.

He asked me what I meant. I was a little surprised because I assumed he'd know being in the business of repetitive movement. I explained the common understanding of muscle memory, but he shook his head. "There's no such thing. Muscles don't remember. The correct term is 'motor memory.'" He went on to explain that motor memory occurs when someone performs correct repetitions of a task, achieving a desired result. That positive feedback is stored in your brain, linked to the physical action that caused it. He was quick to add that cognitive thought still had to occur, which is a great transition to my next point.

By developing and maintaining good situational awareness in order to see pre-incident indicators and relying on attack-recognition skills, you exponentially reduce the likelihood of being surprised or startled, which allows you to THINK if an attack occurs. You'll also appear more alert to the potential threat.

That's a huge advantage; maybe enough of an advantage to adversely affect the criminal's victim-selection process, resulting in him not choosing you as a target in the first place.

COMBATIVES TRAITS AND CHARACTERISTICS

Below are 10 personality traits and characteristics that enable you to deal more effectively with unexpected or unprovoked violence. They're consistently found in people who have developed a combatives mind-set in order to deal with being deployed where there is a high, persistent ambient threat of violence. Dr. Paul Brand, who is a leading provider of comprehensive psychological support programs for companies employing people in war-torn countries, identified these traits and characteristics based on psychological evaluations conducted on thousands of individuals working in theaters of war and hostile areas globally.

I've known Paul for over a decade, and my own government and military training company uses Brand's company, Mission Critical Psychological Services, to screen our own employees for these personality elements. We've spoken often about the importance of screening people to determine whether or not they have the requisite traits and characteristics necessary to operate successfully, either alone or in a team depending on their duties and responsibilities, in high-threat venues. These men need to be counted on in dire circumstances, and proper screening makes sure they can be.

Given an understanding of street violence as I've portrayed it, I hope you clearly see the advantages these traits provide you when you're attacked unexpectedly:

1. **Hardened.** People who have a combatives mind-set are prepared for all possible physical and emotional consequences of their actions. They are ready to engage and will deal with the fallout after the fact. They have a high threshold for physical pain and emotional trauma.

2. **Autonomous.** They do not have a high need for approval or affirmation from others. They act because they feel it is the right thing to do rather than to impress or influence others.

3. **Moral Certitude.** They have already worked out in their mind what is "just cause" for violent action. They are decisive and execute without hesitation.

4. **Adaptable.** They are flexible and willing to break protocol to win. They are opportunists willing to take whatever means are available. In a fight, the focus is on their goal, and they are willing to take a "cheap shot" to meet their objectives.

5. **Confident.** They expect to win even when the odds seem against them. Against bigger or better-armed opponents, they know they can "figure it out."

6. **Courageous.** They are willing to place themselves in harm's way, having already accepted the consequences. They are brave in the worst of circumstances and are eager to take smart risks.

7. **Aggressive.** They assert themselves. They do not wait for things to unfold or escalate too quickly before they take action. They recognize the tactical advantage of proactivity.

8. **Aware.** They have a heightened sense of their environment. They recognize possible dangers before they develop. They possess a good intuitive sense of people's motives. They are not naïve, easily manipulated or swayed.

9. **Thrill seeking.** They have a notable drive for new, unique experiences beyond the norm. They are eager for novel opportunities to challenge their toughness or abilities.

10. **Leadership.** Although they are willing to take direction and embrace missions set by others, they want to take the lead when the opportunity presents itself. This way they will have greater control over events and greater confidence in success.

These traits and characteristics are important. Developing the proper mind-set is equally important in order to deal effectively with violence. Without the proper personality characteristics and mind-set, you may cultivate combatives skills but still fail in the eleventh hour because you can't fight viciously enough.

COMBATIVES MIND-SET

You develop a combatives mind-set based on moral authority. What enables you to act explosively and violently in self-defense is the certainty that you assiduously avoid potentially violent situations and do nothing to provoke attacks. Because you live that way, you have the moral authority to do whatever's necessary to escape without harm when you're confronted by a situation that's a potential threat.

People talk about the mind-set necessary for using combatives, but it's rarely fully explained… so I'll take a stab at it. First, you have to realize the most dangerous men in the world are those who don't hold dear what you do life.

Maybe they don't care about life because of a religious belief or the hopelessness of their personal situation, or maybe it's just the drive to live fast and hard. You can't let consideration of consequence make you so tentative that it diminishes your ability to defend yourself. Remember what my friend Jim Smith (the Marine Raider in Chapter 1) listed as one of his most important characteristics of combatives? Under no circumstance let your mind dwell on possible consequences.

What's essential in situations like these, in my opinion, is focusing on the moment. You've got to unburden yourself of any other responsibility and be free of worry or concern about anything other than prevailing.

Columbian escultas or bodyguards, training in Bogota, Columbia.

A key ingredient to successful operations when attacked is a resolute will to prevail and a combatives mind-set.

Once you're attacked, any opportunity to avoid has passed, so don't waste any time thinking about it. In a weird way, the worse the situation is the better off you may be mentally. When you believe you have a lot of alternative choices but have to select precisely the right one for your survival, you start considering the consequences of each. "If I do that, then I'll be okay…No, that's wrong. If I do the other, then—THEN I'll be okay…"

Conversely, when you believe you're truly screwed and facing a "this is it" moment, you tend to get real clarity of thought. Just DO SOMETHING and do it decisively. The way to take control of the uncertainty, risk and danger present in any unprovoked attack is to cook the fuck off. Race your attacker to the finish. Embrace his goddamned fight. If it's inevitable, you're both going somewhere in this thing. Get there first and crush him.

There are a few more components of a combatives mind-set worth mentioning. Rage is almost always present in victims of unprovoked street attacks. I've always believed there is an element of just bone-deep meanness necessary to fight effectively on the street. Those two things mixed together are a formula for ferocity and fury. Aim it like a handgun and pull the trigger.

The caveat is you need a strong moral compass to rely on. You can't buy one. You've either developed one—based on your upbringing and life experiences—or not. The reason a solid sense of right and wrong is so important is so you'll set limitations on anger and rage and use only the force necessary to stop the threat. Remember, sociopathic criminal personalities are capable of utterly despicable acts because they lack a moral compass.

SO HOW DO I "WIN"?

Having a strong moral compass, you'll recognize when you have a right to defend yourself. It also means you understand your right stops once you've mitigated the threat and controlled the situation. You don't have a right to retribution. Once you're no longer at risk, you're done.

Combatives aren't about winning a competition. Combatives are about prevailing in an unprovoked, violent street attack. Preferably, prevailing means escaping. When escape isn't possible, it means intentionally impairing your attacker to the point you've made him either unwilling or unable to hurt or kill you. It may also mean killing him if you have no other choice.

Any actions you take have to be commensurate with your perception of the level of threat. They must conform to a reasonable use-of-force continuum. I know it's easy to enforce legalities in hindsight after the emergency of an attack is over. Just realize if you're detained as a result of the actions you took in self-defense and the incident is investigated, what you did will be considered in detail by people enjoying the luxury of time—time that didn't exist when you were attacked. You've got to use all the skills I've discussed so far to be as certain as possible your perception of threat is real before launching into physical self-defense.

All of this should reinforce, once again, why it's so important, smart and necessary to be avoidant. That's no small feat when you consider the subtleties and nuances of determining the level of threat you're faced with in a dynamic situation. Here's two examples of what I mean:

Example A

A guy staggers toward you and appears drunk. You try to avoid him but can't. He gets close to you and blocks your path, arresting your movement. Both his hands are in plain view and empty. He grabs your jacket, pulling you into him. In this instance, unless it was a ruse (and you can't know that) the appropriate response would be to:

1. **Create pain.** Don't apply force incrementally but explosively. How? You might use a pain-compliance technique like a clavicle notch, finger jab to his eyes or shin kick to back him off. Note: Shin kick attacks impact the vulnerable nerves running along the tibia. This technique is explained in detail later in the book.

2. **Create space.** When the guy retracts his hand, reacting to the sudden pain you've caused him or retreats altogether, you've created space between you and him.

3. **Exploit for escape.** Use the space you've created to break contact with him and escape.

Example B

The same guy staggers toward you and appears drunk. You try to avoid him but can't. He gets close to you and blocks your path, arresting your movement. He's holding one hand up, chest high, signaling you to stop. You can't see the other hand because it's behind his leg. He reaches toward you to grab your jacket.

This is a completely different circumstance even though the only thing that's changed is you're not able to see both of the guy's hands. Confronted with this situation you've got to assume he may have a weapon and you may be better off:

1. **Acting explosively before he can.** Step to the opposite side of his hidden hand and hook kick him to the ground.

Why is the second situation deserving of such an aggressive response? Because when weapons may be present, you've got to impose a higher standard of control over the situation immediately. The consequence for you if you don't could be far graver than in an unarmed attack.

But remember that control can be achieved not just through traditional trapping, locking and disarming techniques. If you break the assailant's will to use his weapon or make him physically unable to use his weapon, you've controlled him equally well. Regardless, your continual assessment of his ability to be an active aggressor is essential, so if he's still ambulatory and left with the means to be a threat, you've got to finish him more decisively.

Note: Even though I said create pain explosively, that doesn't necessarily mean full power. It means abruptly and fully committed. You can still "pull" power but demonstrate resolute, fearsome intent and achieve the desired result (deterred threat) without laying out some half-wit, unless your assessment leads you to conclude you need to.

CONFRONTATIONS IN REAL LIFE

The process of determining threat level and knowing when a situation is about to become an attack is more art than science. A threat is a potential but as yet unrealized attack. Threats evolve into attacks, sometimes slowly and sometimes abruptly. Once you notice a potential threat through your situational awareness, keep assessing it, enabling you to escape before it fully develops into an attack or to take action at the first indication your risk potential has increased. Sometimes that means choosing to act pre-emptively. The consequence of that choice may have legal ramifications.

For example, in some states, you've got to be able to show you made an effort to retreat from a threat before attacking. In most states (if not all), it's illegal to hit anyone before you're hit or attacked. In order to prevent being thrown in jail as a result of your actions (and you may be), you have to be able to precisely articulate what made you feel threatened and why you felt you were in jeopardy or why you feared for your life.

You'll either get pissed off about this mess and say, "Fuck that, I know what I'm gonna do! A guy threatens me and I'll have his ass!" Or you're starting to understand why it's smart to use situational awareness and attack-recognition skills to be avoidant before beating someone senseless.

In a lot of instances when you use force, you avoid physical consequences only to be confronted with legal consequences. Acting lawfully with awareness helps avoid this catch-22, but things can still get really complicated. If, for example, you exercise your right to self-defense by using too much force or an illegal or illegally concealed weapon, then you're still in trouble. If you have to use force, continual assessment of the effect your techniques are having on an attacker is crucial. It avoids the gratuitous use of violence. You're not justified in using excessive force just because you're amped, pissed and determined to get a pound of flesh out of your attacker.

Threats aren't usually this obvious until they are. Seeing subtle indications that a threat is developing may enable you to avoid ugliness like this.

What I'm trying to impress on you is that none of this is peel-and-stick easy.

I'll end this section of the book with a true-life assault that happened in 2006. My friend Kevin got in a jam while vacationing in Central Europe from a deployment in Africa. I asked him if he would describe the incident in an e-mail so I could conclude this section with it. He agreed.

Your use of force to defend yourself must be justified in regard to the level of threat offered to you. Gratuitous violence is illegal.

Kelly,

Sorry to take so long to respond but here's the pertinent info. I apologize for the lack of coherency. I'm surprised I still get angry over it after all this time. If you have any questions, please call.

On vacation in Central Europe, I was targeted in an attempted mugging.

I was leaving a nightclub, returning to my hotel late at night, when I was approached by two men. One approached me directly from the front and stopped within a foot of me while the other was off to my right side at about a 45-degree angle and at arm's length. The one in front asked me for money. When I refused, he brandished a large knife similar to a butcher's deboning knife and demanded I give him my wallet. I was carrying a folding knife in my right rear pocket.

Photo courtesy of Kelly McCann

A 10-inch boning knife similar to the one used to attack Kevin.

I reached back—I'm sure he thought I was getting my wallet—pulled my knife and thrust it straight into the neck of the assailant to my front. I didn't have a good grip on the handle and wasn't able to withdraw the blade after my thrust. He dropped his knife after I struck. Thinking the second man was probably armed, I attempted an ax hand, when I couldn't pull my knife out, but didn't deliver an effective strike. The second man tried to pick up the knife his partner had dropped, and I was able to knee him in his ribs, preventing him from getting to it. I picked it up and attacked him with multiple slashes and thrusts as he came at me, primarily to his midsection.

I'm fortunate I survived as I made several mistakes. First, I had separated from my buddy at the nightclub. Second, I'd been drinking. Lastly, I was in a city I didn't know well enough to be walking around alone that late at night.

I think the thing that saved me was training I had in the Corps and the combatives training in my career afterwards. I had the ability to get into the right mental state instantly, deciding to act with overwhelming violence.

I had a hard time dealing with the aftermath of this event as both men died from their wounds. I was and am still angry these guys caused it. I've also asked myself many times if I hadn't been out alone that late would it have happened at all? And could I have disabled them without killing them? Once again though, the training I've had in combatives, particularly in having the right mind-set, helped greatly.

Talking with friends who have dealt with similar issues and situations helped me deal with the fallout.

Semper Fi,

Kevin

Both attackers were in their mid-20s. The first attacker was carrying the knife beneath a large coat, drew it and held it at Kevin's belt line. Kevin doesn't remember opening his knife, only reaching for it and then thrusting. The first attacker buckled, dropped and died where he stood after Kevin stabbed him in the throat (just under the jawline at an upward angle). The second attacker was shocked and stood motionless until Kevin turned toward him, throwing an ax hand. When he advanced on Kevin, his intent to continue the attack became clear. Kevin stabbed and slashed his midsection several times. The attacker fled the scene and died a short distance away.

Kevin stayed where he was, put the attacker's knife—which he used to kill the second man—down on the ground and called for the police. They arrived on scene quickly. Kevin stood in place, hands up, palms outward and followed police instructions.

The police recognized the slain criminals as bad men with current outstanding arrest warrants. They brought Kevin to the nearest police station and began interviewing him. Meanwhile, on-scene investigators noticed a surveillance camera covering the attack location. They recovered the video, which revealed Kevin had clearly been approached by two men—one who was armed—in an attempted armed robbery. It was also apparent the second attacker attempted to recover his partner's dropped knife instead of escaping when the opportunity presented itself, indicating he was still an active aggressor. In light of both attackers' known criminal dispositions and the videotape of the assault, Kevin was released. He suffered no injuries.

He told me that during the assault, he'd experienced most of the physiological effects of imminent danger. Kevin's a big guy who is skilled in combatives and trains regularly with us. He reported tunnel vision, auditory exclusion, visual slowdown (when dealing with the second attacker), "seeing red" or "feeling dazzled," palpitations, tremors and shortness of breath. He added that the dazzle effect lasted for some time—approximately 10 to 15 minutes after the attack.

It's interesting that having safely operated in a country regarded as one of the most dangerous in Africa, Kevin was attacked in a benign country known for safe tourism. That's why situational awareness is a fundamental necessity regardless of where you are. I've said it over and over: When it comes to street violence, the only thing you can be certain of is uncertainty.

Despite being a combat veteran and experienced operator, the fact that the incident took place at all troubles Kevin to this day.

PART II

COMBATIVES ARE RELENTLESS.

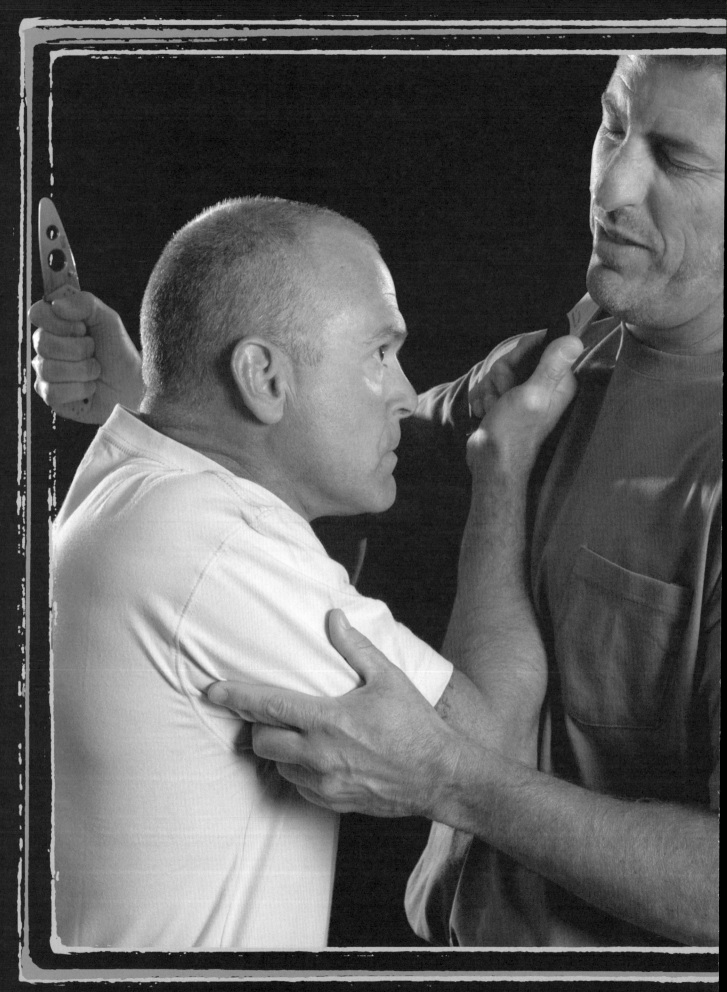

CHAPTER 3
COMBATIVES PRINCIPLES

Combatives principles are a set of rules applied in every self-defense situation to ensure the effectiveness of your movements and strikes. Focusing on them in training develops your combatives skills faster and more efficiently than if you focus on technique alone.

You'll find these principles are interrelated and mutually supporting. Cumulatively, they make you much more efficient when you fight. Apply them universally, and you'll gain significant advantages over an attacker.

PRINCIPLE NO. 1: GO ARMED

This should be an obvious concept. No matter how skilled you are, the use of any type of weapon provides you a significant advantage.

Quality Purpose-Built Weapons

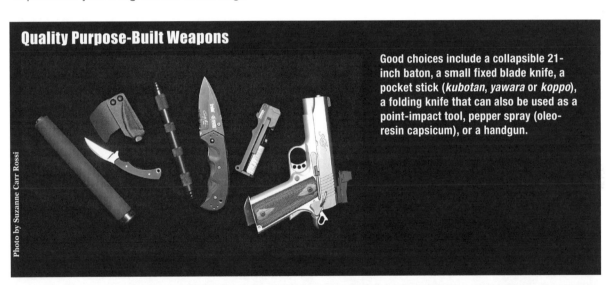

Photo by Suzanne Carr Rossi

Good choices include a collapsible 21-inch baton, a small fixed blade knife, a pocket stick (*kubotan*, *yawara* or *koppo*), a folding knife that can also be used as a point-impact tool, pepper spray (oleo-resin capsicum), or a handgun.

Being Armed is a Mind-Set

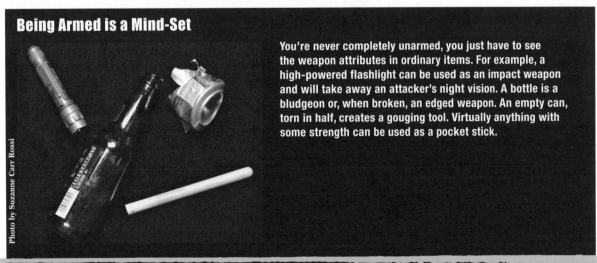

Photo by Suzanne Carr Rossi

You're never completely unarmed, you just have to see the weapon attributes in ordinary items. For example, a high-powered flashlight can be used as an impact weapon and will take away an attacker's night vision. A bottle is a bludgeon or, when broken, an edged weapon. An empty can, torn in half, creates a gouging tool. Virtually anything with some strength can be used as a pocket stick.

The most important thing about any weapon is that it acts as a trigger when coupled with good situational awareness and attack-recognition skills. When you find yourself reaching for your weapon, it triggers heightened situational awareness, compelling your immediate escape from the situation.

In my opinion, if you don't arm yourself with a legally concealed weapon or an improvised weapon when necessary, you're negligent. When's it necessary? If you knew, you could schedule when to carry a weapon and when not to. You should *always* carry a weapon or an item that can be used as a weapon. Period. Arm yourself with a weapon that can be legally carried in the jurisdiction where you live.

PRINCIPLE NO. 2: AVOID OFFENSIVELY

Always prefer to avoid confrontations rather than fight in self-defense, but once a threat evolves into an attack, you've got to respond with a resolute, offensive mind-set. The second you perceive an attack is underway, become the attacker. Pre-empt the assault and immediately reverse the confrontational dynamic.

Why? Because it's easier to make your attacker react to you than trying to react to him. Action is always faster than reaction. It's much more effective to force your attacker to continually try and catch up to you than the reverse. It's how you TAKE control away from him.

See the Attacker...Be the Attacker

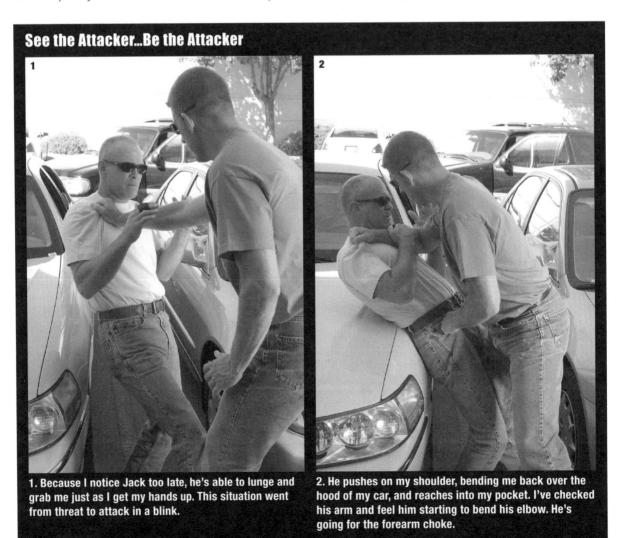

1. Because I notice Jack too late, he's able to lunge and grab me just as I get my hands up. This situation went from threat to attack in a blink.

2. He pushes on my shoulder, bending me back over the hood of my car, and reaches into my pocket. I've checked his arm and feel him starting to bend his elbow. He's going for the forearm choke.

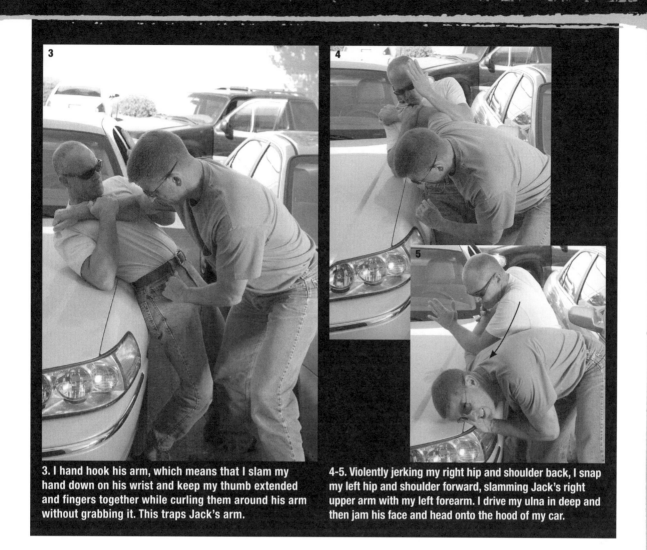

3. I hand hook his arm, which means that I slam my hand down on his wrist and keep my thumb extended and fingers together while curling them around his arm without grabbing it. This traps Jack's arm.

4-5. Violently jerking my right hip and shoulder back, I snap my left hip and shoulder forward, slamming Jack's right upper arm with my left forearm. I drive my ulna in deep and then jam his face and head onto the hood of my car.

Don't confuse the application of this principle with trying to anticipate *specifically* what your attacker's going to do. It's enough to just know he's going to attack when you're pre-empting. Many martial arts promote the idea of anticipation—anticipating which hand an attacker is going to strike with, for example. The problem with that approach is the high cost of anticipating *incorrectly*. If you anticipate an attacker's going to throw a right-handed haymaker (a wild looping punch at the head), but he throws a left jab straight down the middle instead, then you're screwed.

Remember, the best self-defense is explosive self-offense.

PRINCIPLE NO. 3: CLEAR YOUR BODY OF THE ATTACK

If you're facing your attacker, get out of his way when he charges you. John Styers called these "in-quartata" or out-of-line movements. They're common in fencing, bayonet drills and boxing.

Colloquially, I refer to the movement as "opening the gate" because it's a more effective visual reference for students. When an attacker charges the gate (you), open it and let him through. It's a simple, fast movement that incorporates a stiff arm (face mash) or fend (keeping his hands from grabbing your clothing) as you move out of line.

Don't cross your legs. Sweep either foot backward in an arc until your hips and shoulders are perpendicular to his direction of attack, then *immediately* counterattack "in line" or straight ahead.

Get Out of the Way

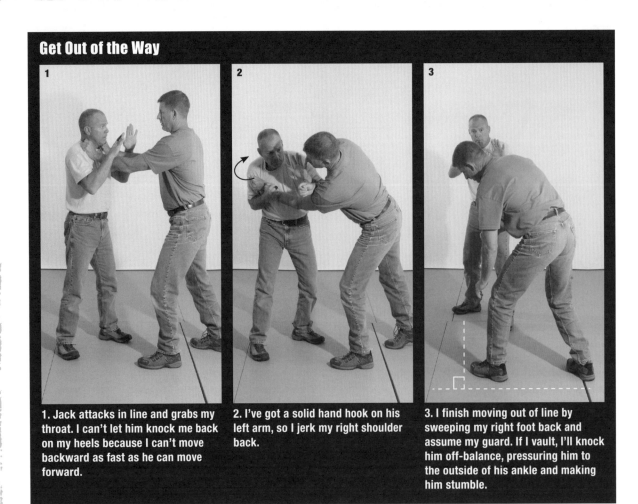

1. Jack attacks in line and grabs my throat. I can't let him knock me back on my heels because I can't move backward as fast as he can move forward.

2. I've got a solid hand hook on his left arm, so I jerk my right shoulder back.

3. I finish moving out of line by sweeping my right foot back and assume my guard. If I vault, I'll knock him off-balance, pressuring him to the outside of his ankle and making him stumble.

Clearing your body of the path of any weapon (the attacker himself, his fist, knife or stick) is a fundamental combatives principle. Get out of your attacker's way and immediately counterattack him on a perpendicular angle, forcing his center of gravity to the outside of his ankles. This rapid combination of movement will usually result in him stumbling as he tries to regain his balance.

PRINCIPLE NO. 4: APPLY POWER EXPLOSIVELY

Combatives techniques are applied explosively; the power in each is delivered all at once not gradually. It's the difference between using an on/off light switch and a dimmer switch. When you throw your on/off switch, the sudden pain of your technique overwhelms an attacker and creates unintentional reactions. Conversely, if you used a dimmer, your technique would gradually build in intensity, giving the attacker the opportunity to adapt.

Make your attacker react unintentionally to sudden and excruciating pain. Then immediately exploit it and any other vulnerability. You can't reliably predict *what* his reaction will be, so don't anticipate it. Just be prepared to exploit *any* reaction you see.

Put Your Attacker in Hot Water

1-2. Seeing my hands are full and that I'm preoccupied with opening my trunk, Jack rushes me from behind. He slips on a full nelson and prepares to bounce my face off the trunk. I drop my bags immediately to free up my hands.

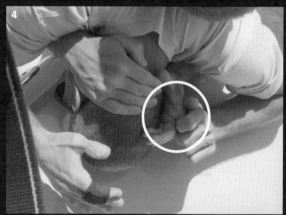

3-4. I use both my hands to pry just one of his fingers up, making it impossible for him to resist. I then secure it with just my left hand.

5-6. Once I've secured his finger, I don't alert him to what I'm going to do by applying gradual strain against it. He might wrestle it free. Instead, I explode and jerk it back, breaking his finger and setting him up for my next attack. Wow, looks like that hurt.

PRINCIPLE NO. 5: ESCAPE THROUGH PAIN-INDUCED PATHWAYS

Creating sudden, sharp pain in your attacker usually results in an uncontrollable, instinctive reaction of some kind, like snatching his hand back or releasing his grip. His reaction will be similar to being touched with a lit match. A reaction to pain creates opportunities—usually space—between you and your attacker that can be exploited in different ways to support your escape. You've got the option to:

- reassess your situation because he jerks away creating some distance between the two of you.
- escape because he releases his grip on you.
- attack because he suddenly stops when you disrupt his assault.

Making Space

When he grabbed my left arm unexpectedly, Jack initially had the momentum advantage. Using my hips and shoulders for power, I nail him in his pectoral muscle, driving my closed telescoping baton deep. Jack can't let go fast enough, giving me the opportunity and space I need to escape.

My old man used to say, "If you touch a man, you can hurt him," and it's especially true with an implement in your hand. The immediate result of striking Jack with a baton is obvious: He lets go of my arm, leans back and is off-balance. He's not thinking about smacking me in the face. A split second ago, Jack had the momentum, but because I created pain, Jack created space.

PRINCIPLE NO. 6: USE THE RIGHT WEAPON

Your body is made up of personal weapons. Your hands, elbows, knees and feet can all be used efficiently during a fight. In order to be a comprehensive combatives practitioner, you have to learn to maximize the effectiveness of every strike without injuring yourself in the process.

The types of strikes you execute with your personal weapons can be broadly categorized as: head strikes, penetrating soft-tissue strikes and structural strikes.

Head strikes are attacks on the head intended to knock your attacker unconscious. If you're trying to knock someone out, you want to transfer as much energy as possible into his head. So use a soft weapon. What?!?! That's right, a soft weapon. Your slack, open hand coupled with full body-weight striking is more likely to knock someone out than a fist. As an added benefit, you probably won't break a small finger bone like the metacarpal from punching without properly positioning your hand or locking your wrist. This is known as a "brawler's fracture" and is a common street-fighting injury.

Look, although no one knows definitively what causes knockouts, the most prevalent school of thought is that rapid acceleration of the head, not necessarily from a direct impact, causes rotational and/or angular movement of the brain within the skull. This movement results in the momentary disruption of normal brain function or a knockout and potential concussion. Open-hand strikes in combatives—like the face mash, cupped hand or chin jab—maximize each element of knocking someone out. They cause rapid rotational or angular movement by transferring tremendous energy into the head.

One example is a technique some combatives guys call the "bear paw" or "bear slap." Some even call it a "bitch slap." It's a gross-motor open-hand slap to an attacker's head. On contact, you follow through, continuing to drive your hand into his head and transferring the maximum amount of energy through it. No matter what you call it or which weapon you apply the principle with, the effectiveness of striking the head with soft weapons can't be argued.

Headshot

1-2. The rotational impact to Jack's head is really apparent in these photos. All the kinetic energy of my strike is explosively deposited directly into his head, snapping it back and to the side.

Soft-tissue strikes are intended to create pain by penetrating deep into soft tissue, causing trauma by striking nerve centers. Use hard or bony weapons like the ulna, a fist or the point of an elbow to effectively penetrate into your attacker's soft tissue.

Penetrating Strikes

1. Despite hammerfisting Jack, I'm still locked between his legs. So I posture up to chamber my elbows…

2. …and drive them down into his femoral nerves to get them unlocked.

Structural strikes are attacks made on the attacker's knees using destructive kicks. They're intended to break his "base." Destroying the structure that holds him up is useful to lower his height so you can attack him more efficiently, unbalance him and render him nonambulatory.

Breaking Base

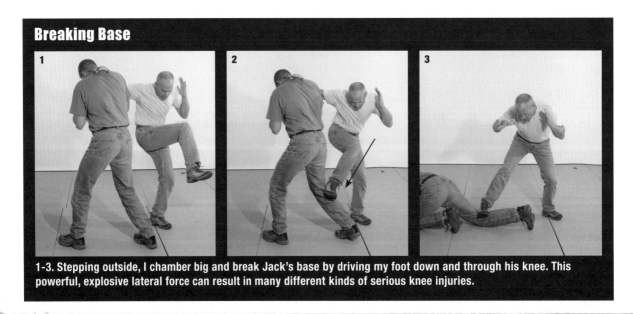

1-3. Stepping outside, I chamber big and break Jack's base by driving my foot down and through his knee. This powerful, explosive lateral force can result in many different kinds of serious knee injuries.

What you want to achieve determines which personal weapon you use to deliver a particular strike to a particular target. For example, I'd rather hit the side of my attacker's neck or the base of his skull with an elbow instead of his face because I'd prefer to knock him out and not just cut him open.

Don't confuse this with precision. Combatives are about hitting more often and with more power than your attacker. In order to do this, you've got to ensure you select the right personal weapon for the job and rely on gross-motor movements to execute them with.

PRINCIPLE NO. 7: RELY ON GROSS-MOTOR MOVEMENTS

The physiological effects of imminent danger cause duress dysfunctions, making fine-motor-movement techniques difficult if not impossible. Combatives techniques are made up of gross-motor movements resulting in you being far less affected by startle and your body's natural responses to danger. Subsequently, you'll be less diminished by duress and consequently will be more able to effectively defend yourself.

Gross-Motor Simplicity

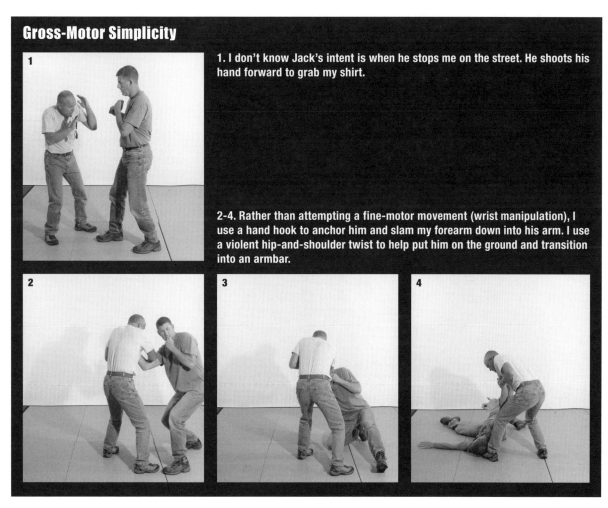

1. I don't know Jack's intent is when he stops me on the street. He shoots his hand forward to grab my shirt.

2-4. Rather than attempting a fine-motor movement (wrist manipulation), I use a hand hook to anchor him and slam my forearm down into his arm. I use a violent hip-and-shoulder twist to help put him on the ground and transition into an armbar.

I concentrate on attacking rather than on something Jack hasn't even tried yet. Instead, I just hit him. Keeping my plan simple and using uncomplicated techniques, I think clearly and don't get muddled considering what he *might* do.

PRINCIPLE NO. 8: BUILD AND CRASH THE GAP

Continuously build gaps—space or distance—between you and your attacker to increase the power of your elbows and knees. How? Maintain control of him and shove him away from yourself to build the gap. If you can't push him away, push yourself away. Then, violently jerk him back into your strikes, i.e. crash it. If you can't, yank yourself back into him, leading with a knee or elbow strike. If you don't create gaps, your strikes end up just pushing against your attacker rather than impacting on him.

The worst type of car crash is a head-on collision when the aggregate closing speed of both vehicles is much greater than in any other crash. Continually create head-on collisions when you fight. You may be wondering, "Yeah, but wouldn't we both get hurt equally?" No. Because in this human example of a car crash, you're colliding your knee or elbow with his unprotected face, ribs, groin or thoracic cavity. Visualize each strike as a violent car crash.

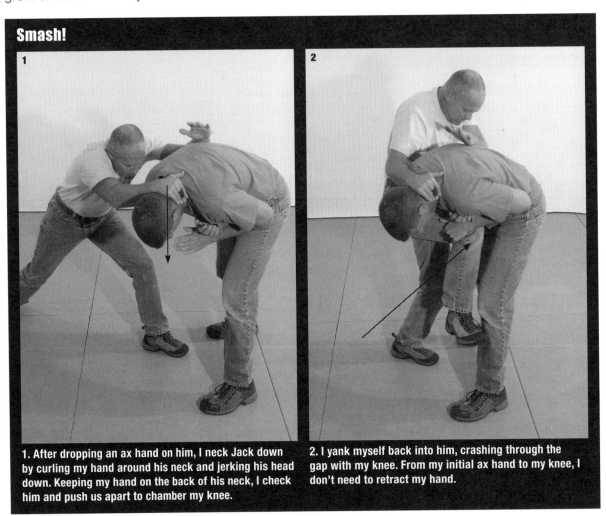

Smash!

1. After dropping an ax hand on him, I neck Jack down by curling my hand around his neck and jerking his head down. Keeping my hand on the back of his neck, I check him and push us apart to chamber my knee.

2. I yank myself back into him, crashing through the gap with my knee. From my initial ax hand to my knee, I don't need to retract my hand.

Continuously jerking an attacker into your strikes helps establish your control and dominance over him by keeping him off-balance. Don't just jerk him around; that'll deteriorate into a struggle and doesn't hurt him. It's what you jerk him *into* that hurts.

PRINCIPLE NO. 9: FULL BODY-WEIGHT STRIKING

Fighting is partly the application of physics. In the simplest terms, the combination of more mass that moves at a higher velocity over a longer distance equals greater impact. To take advantage of this basic formula, you have to maximize each variable in it.

1. **More mass.** Always strike with your whole body and not just a limb. Exploding off your rear foot in the direction of your strike is called vaulting and is far more powerful than standing in place and only striking with your arm. It doesn't matter what hits your attacker—a knee, elbow, fist or open hand—as long as it conforms to the principle of choosing the correct personal weapon. Violence of action and putting your body weight behind each strike is critical to generating power. Do it over and over until it becomes habit.

2. **More velocity.** Vaulting is explained in detail in Chapter 5. It's an essential technique to amplify the speed that your body crashes into an attacker. It's fearsome for an attacker to see and experience you literally exploding off your back foot and into him. You don't *step* into the attack—you fucking *detonate* into it.

3. **Over longer distance.** Build a gap like I told you.

Strikes with Some Ass Behind Them

1-2. I push off my foot in the direction of my strike, attacking with my whole body. All my weight will drop into the ax hand to make it exponentially more powerful than if I stood stationary and only used my arm to strike.

Here's some more tips on full body-weight striking:

- **Stay loose.** Consciously avoid tightening up. Breathe. Be a little sloppy. Fighting's not demonstrating a form for points. When you stiffen up your hand, speed is detrimentally affected and so is your reaction speed. Visualize your attack on the attacker; it helps lower your anxiety level.

- **Vault in the direction of your strike.** Don't step forward *pulling* your weight behind you. Instead, *explode* off your rearmost foot to propel yourself into the strike. Visualize attacking with your whole body.
- **Develop your footwork and timing.** Ensure your weight *drops* into your strikes on impact as your lead foot lands. With some practice, combatives footwork and timing becomes second nature and won't require any thought.
- **Load and unload violently.** In addition to the simple formula of more mass at a greater velocity over a longer distance, involve your hips and shoulders when you strike. Maximize the kinetic-energy transfer into what you strike using rotational torque. You generate torque by twisting and then untwisting your hips and shoulders.
- **Visualize every strike passing through the attacker.** No matter what strike you throw, visualize it exiting out the other side of your attacker like a bullet. If you don't, you'll unnecessarily limit the depth of your strike, resulting in a surface impact rather than a penetrating strike.

PRINCIPLE NO. 10: REPETITIVE STRIKING

Repetitive striking is called "cycling" and is simply quickly repeating the same strike two or three times to exploit success. So if you stagger your attacker with a right-hand hammerfist, you'd chamber it again as your left hand (your "offhand") smashes into his face. Retract your offhand and smash his face with your hammerfist again, then slam your offhand back into his face and so on. Repetitive striking is a finishing technique effective with hammerfists, slashing elbows and knees.

Some strikes don't lend themselves to being cycled very well. For example, you can't efficiently cycle a chin jab; it wouldn't work ergonomically. Besides if you've gotten the chin jab right, you won't need to. Your attacker should be horizontal in the air. The fight's over.

Cycling strikes is as much about ferocity and intensity as it is about effectiveness. If you're moving as fast and efficiently as you should be when throwing a slashing elbow, you'll stay married to your attacker's chest, keeping him within range even as he falls away. You'll have plenty of time to land one or two more strikes before he hits the deck.

It's not exactly a straight blast or a *kempo* technique in which both hands strike. In combatives, cycling means letting your most powerful hand do the hitting and putting your offhand to work, just differently than your strong hand.

Jack Hammer

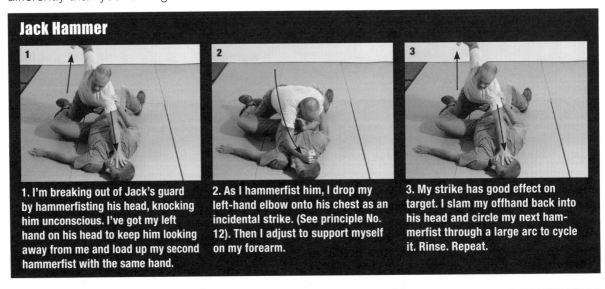

1. I'm breaking out of Jack's guard by hammerfisting his head, knocking him unconscious. I've got my left hand on his head to keep him looking away from me and load up my second hammerfist with the same hand.

2. As I hammerfist him, I drop my left-hand elbow onto his chest as an incidental strike. (See principle No. 12). Then I adjust to support myself on my forearm.

3. My strike has good effect on target. I slam my offhand back into his head and circle my next hammerfist through a large arc to cycle it. Rinse. Repeat.

Visualize your striking hand or elbow and your offhand as pistons attached to a camshaft—your shoulders. As one piston reaches top dead center, the other reaches its lowest point. As the first starts to descend, the other ascends with equal force. And so on, over and over again.

Both my hands are working—one hammerfists while the other face mashes or checks. No matter what, while one hand cycles, your offhand should be doing something—disrupting vision, jerking....

PRINCIPLE NO. 11: ALTERNATE HIGH AND LOW STRIKES

If all your strikes are aimed above your attacker's waist, he'll concentrate his defenses there, diminishing your effectiveness. Instead, overwhelm him with high and low strikes. Make him react so he's always one step behind you and unable to catch up. Put him on the defensive and keep him there. Strike him high with a slashing elbow then, when he reacts, shin kick his ass. When he reacts to the shin kick, close the deal with a hammerfist to his head.

Don't misunderstand the application of this principle as contradictory to cycling. Cycling is used to exploit success when you've hurt your attacker and smell blood. Alternate high and low strikes to keep your attacker guessing where the next shot is coming from. His uncertainty, confusion and frustration sets up the opening for the strike that'll stagger him, giving you the opportunity to cycle and finish him.

I've Been Up...I've Been Down...

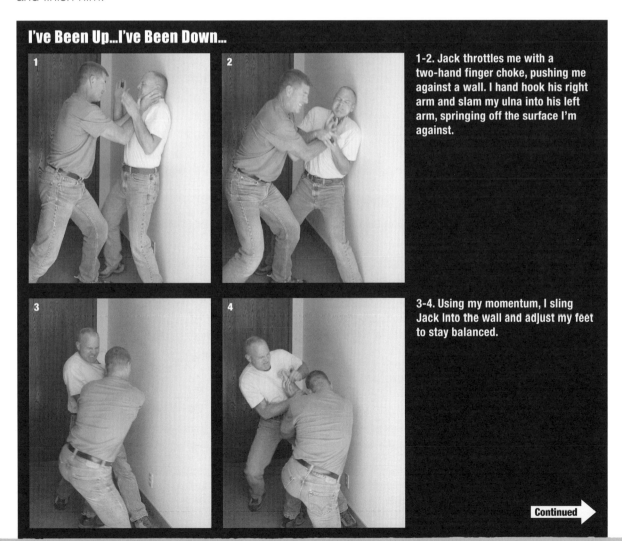

1-2. Jack throttles me with a two-hand finger choke, pushing me against a wall. I hand hook his right arm and slam my ulna into his left arm, springing off the surface I'm against.

3-4. Using my momentum, I sling Jack into the wall and adjust my feet to stay balanced.

Continued →

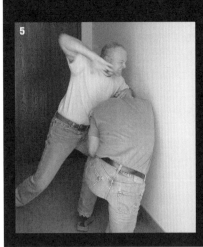

5-6. I fire off a vicious elbow to the back of his head. Then while controlling his head, I crash the gap with my chambered knee and try to break every rib on Jack's left side.

The sequence ends with me alternating between a high and low strike, but notice how I've applied many other combatives principles as well. I used full body-weight striking, applied power explosively, used the right personal weapon and kept all my techniques gross motor.

By the way, in case you hadn't figured it out, high line means above the waist and low line means below the waist.

PRINCIPLE NO. 12: INCIDENTAL STRIKING

If you can touch a man, you can hurt him, right? Incidental strikes simply fill brief voids that occur during a fight, making your overall attack more comprehensive. They keep your attacker reacting to pain, on the defensive and increasingly desperate to cover up in order to stop the damage.

If you're struggling with an attacker and you both fall to the ground, try to land on him with your weight on the points of your elbows and knees; you want them to crush into him. Smash your hands down into his face for support when you scramble to get up. Anytime you reach past your attacker's face, smack it with the heel of your palm or drag your fingers through his eyes.

Ah, Incidentally... Examples

1. I'm posturing up on Jack and see the opportunity to use an incidental technique to keep him in pain. I jam my elbow on his neck along the jawline to get up. This not only hurts him but keeps him facing away from me.

2. Jack grabs me from behind and tries to run me face first into the wall. I lift my elbow tip as I turn around accomplishing two things: I get myself out of Jack's line of attack and may just incidentally clip his head or face.

3. I support myself on my elbow tip, digging it into Jack's chest and creating some sharp pain for him to deal with while I get into a position to strike.

You get the picture. Don't try to create opportunities for incidental strikes as that would just distract you from finding a way to finish and open up your guard. (I discuss the guard in Chapter 5). All you've got to do is remember to jump on any chance—big or small—to hurt your attacker.

PRINCIPLE NO. 13: UNARMED DOUBLE TAPS

To capitalize on momentary opportunities that occur when blocking, I adapted a bayonet fighting technique John Styers developed called the "beat." He taught Marines to knock the enemy's rifle down using their own rifle with a sharp, fast "beat," and then to immediately follow up with a thrust into the enemy's face, eyes or throat.

I adapted this fast, fractional movement to unarmed combat for blocking and striking, fusing them. Like a double tap in combat shooting, the two actions are linked; they become fractional and not separate whole movements. BaBoom instead of Boom. Boom.

This technique is super fast, effective and reliable.

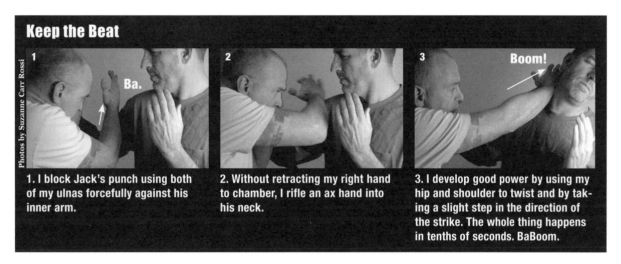

Keep the Beat

Photos by Suzanne Carr Rossi

1. I block Jack's punch using both of my ulnas forcefully against his inner arm.

2. Without retracting my right hand to chamber, I rifle an ax hand into his neck.

3. I develop good power by using my hip and shoulder to twist and by taking a slight step in the direction of the strike. The whole thing happens in tenths of seconds. BaBoom.

PRINCIPLE NO. 14: RAGE WITH REASON

Don't just "lose" it in a fight. That's dangerous because without the ability to continually assess developments—the introduction of a weapon for example, alerting on the arrival of more attackers or maybe avoiding an environmental obstacle like a trip hazard—you could suffer the same fate as the felon in the beginning of the book. Remember? He was in such a violent rage he didn't realize his victim had pulled a knife.

It's also dangerous because you may not be able to reel your rage in. Not good—the end of that story might be sitting in court waiting to hear if a jury of your peers found you guilty of using excessive force in self-defense.

Listen, we're NOT "sharing a moment" here with knowing winks and nods or a nudge in the ribs and a smirk. Investigatory techniques and forensics are far too sophisticated, and there are way too many cameras around to think you'll get away with inappropriate or excessive use of force. To want to would be morally *bankrupt.*

Retribution is neither lawful nor your right. You've only the right to defend yourself within a use-of-force continuum, which is using the appropriate level of force to stop the threat presented to you, and no more. DO THE RIGHT THING or you may find yourself sitting in the can with all your new convict buddies wishing you had.

Whoa!

STOP RIGHT THERE! Jack's not a threat anymore. He's out cold on the ground. Sure, I'm pissed he attacked me, but once I've controlled the threat I'm done.

CHAPTER 4
COMBATIVES METHODOLOGY

Training in combatives means learning how to train combatively. Since combatives prepares you to defend yourself, you have to train under conditions that are accurate reflections of street situations. In this chapter, I'll discuss how to use power and speed safely, how to organize and conduct combatives training and how to protect yourself while you train.

TO BANG OR NOT TO BANG—HOW HARD IS HARD ENOUGH

*B*lack Belt Executive Editor Robert W. Young said this in his June 2008 editorial column on watching Jack and I bang for a photo shoot:

"McCann [and] Jack Stradley went at it like a couple of velociraptors. By the time the shoot was over, both were bleeding, and Stradley must surely have suffered some internal injuries. I repeatedly reminded them that they were performing for a still camera and could slow the action down [but] McCann said they couldn't because of the way their style of combatives is taught and practiced."

A question that invariably comes up is: "How hard should I bang?" My honest answer is: "As hard as you can stand it," followed by, "but use some common sense."

When you're impact training on each other, how hard you strike depends on the technique, the scenario, the sequence, the weapon, whether you're wearing any protective equipment and, most importantly, you and your training partners' appetites for intensity. In any case, you need to really think about how to blast safely. The good news is applying a few precautions and adhering to some simple guidance keeps your training as safe as combatives training can be.

For example, if you're working on unarmed-defense-against-edged-weapons drills, the "attacker" should wear protective equipment specific to those drills, which we'll discuss later in this chapter. But he should slash and thrust at you with full power and speed. By training at this level of speed, power and intensity, you'll develop a true appreciation for what it takes—for real—to defend against an attacker who's slashing and stabbing at you on the street.

The same is true for pistol disarms. Although some pistol-disarming techniques look like they work, they fail to ensure the most important thing: that you move yourself out of the weapon's line of attack FIRST. The bad guy may squeeze one off because of poor weapons handling, sympathetic muscle tightening due to a startle or because of the other variables present in these situations. You've

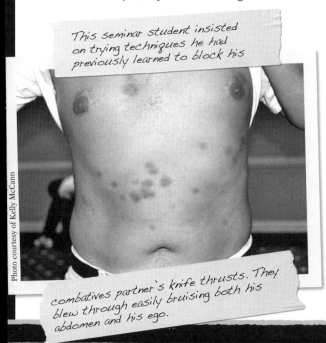

This seminar student insisted on trying techniques he had previously learned to block his combatives partner's knife thrusts. They blew through easily bruising both his abdomen and his ego.

Photo courtesy of Kelly McCann

got to be sure you don't catch it in your face, chest or abdomen. You're very likely to be shot using techniques developed by people who aren't experienced with firearms and have no firsthand experience with close firearm attacks.

On a side note, training as hard as you're able is the acid test lacking in a lot of disarming techniques people believe are streetworthy. I've seen hundreds of techniques for disarming over the years. Some look great until you attempt them under more realistic conditions. That's when they fall apart. For example, you may learn pretty quickly that you're likely to break your fingers trying to catch your training partner's knife-hand wrist or that you just CAN'T catch it.

Back on point, using as much force as I'm suggesting in training gets a bit complicated when you're working sequences with two or three individual techniques linked together. Here's why: Different types of strikes are going to hit different anatomical points on your partner's body. This means that during one sequence you may have to regulate your force several different ways yet still maintain overall ferocity and intensity.

For example, let's say the sequence you're working on is a right-foot shin kick, followed by a right slashing elbow and finished with an ankle stomp. Suit your partner up in a baseball catcher's shin guard to absorb the shin-kick impact and maybe a cervical collar to protect his neck (if he doesn't have a solid guard position). Make sure your training partner keeps his leg slightly bent so the force of the kick doesn't hyperextend his knee. When you cook off, blast the shin kick. Then fire your elbow, targeting the base of his skull. However, as it lands, pull significant power—but not speed—from the strike because the base of his skull is very vulnerable. Crank off your full power ankle stomp and land it to the side—near but not on—his ankle.

As training starts to intensify, you and your partner will get really amped. The action gets more dynamic, harder to control and the potential for injury increases significantly. BE CAREFUL. You can't afford accidentally planting these kinds of strikes on anyone you don't intend to hurt badly.

Watch It!

You have to *make sure*, if you're going to *plant* the stomp, there's no chance of it landing on your training partner. The damage caused by a stomp like this on a joint could be irreversible, crippling Jack for life.

Big boy rules apply when you train aggressively. It's important everyone understands the *very* real risk of serious injury—not just split lips and bloody noses—and work together to create the safest, most realistic and hard-core training experience.

Whoever is fulfilling the role of an attacker should be animated, forcing his partner to develop his skill in perceiving threats and exploiting opportunities as quickly as they occur. At the same time, whoever's fulfilling the role of victim has to execute his technique hard enough to actually take control of the role-playing attacker. "Hard enough" results in the role-playing attacker becoming less animated because the confrontational dynamic has been reversed, just like it would on the street.

The goal is to replicate what actually happens on the street in the same amount of time and with the same intensity but without the same consequences.

If you've never trained this way, it's difficult at first. But in my opinion, the closer you train at full speed, power and intensity, the sooner you'll develop truly useful combatives skills.

TRAINING GROUND RULES

Training like this can be tricky because a lot of people are uncomfortable at first with the intensity. Don't take it personally when the violence gets cranked up—it isn't, but it is reciprocal. I'm going to bang on my partner as hard as I *expect* him to bang on me. We're going to push each other as hard as each of us is willing and able. If you get stuck with a partner who isn't as motivated to wick it up, keep switching partners until you find a kindred spirit.

Over the years, I've established some ground rules that maintain order and keep things from potentially getting out of hand. They hold people individually accountable for their own and each other's safety, ensuring that training is intense but relatively injury-free.

1. **No one gets to watch.** If you show up, you're training. This rule reduces the performance pressure felt by students as they learn and attempt new, unfamiliar techniques. No one likes to do anything they're not good at—looking and feeling a little foolish until their skills improve. If everyone's sharing the challenges, getting sweaty and banged up, no one feels self-conscious. FNGs get embarrassed in front of people who aren't training and just watching and rightfully so; there's no comparison between holding a wall up with your ass and trying to hold your head up on the mat.

   By the way, instructors are not excused from training. No preening or prancing prima donnas allowed. After demonstrating a technique, instructors should crank some reps alongside their students *then* prowl the mat. It maintains credibility and provides another opportunity for students to watch, learn and then execute techniques. Everyone is subjected to each other's scrutiny. Everyone sweats. Everyone bruises. *Everyone* bleeds.

2. **Save the cheap shots for the street.** If you've been training awhile, you've no doubt run into the guy who loves to let one rip and then immediately apologizes, "Ooops! I'm sorry man. You okay? Sorry…" But then it happens again and then again. Don't let anyone get away with that in your training group. Sure everybody slips up once in awhile; it's inevitable. But this guy? This guy, you promptly knock on his ass when it's your turn. Give it back to him equally as hard as he gave it to you without the apology. He'll get the hint.

   When everyone understands gratuitous smackdowns aren't tolerated and that excessive force is reciprocal, unpleasant situations just don't seem to develop.

3. Stick to the drill. In other words, don't trick-fuck your partner. Stick to the drill as demonstrated and directed. If you're the role-playing attacker working with a partner fending high-line strikes, then you throw high-line strikes. But let's say you close on your partner and throw a low-line shin kick to set up your high-line strike…you should pay for that. We have a saying: "If someone gets out of line, redline." What it means is if you go offline like doing something in a drill you weren't directed to do, your partner gets to go offline, too. When everyone's training hard, there's a real potential for injury. Don't increase that potential unnecessarily. Save your creativity for freestyle when it's appropriate.

4. ALWAYS protect yourself. Sometimes training gets pretty crazy, especially during duress drills. It's everyone's personal responsibility to protect themselves. The result could be tragic if a student's depth perception is off by just a few inches when executing an ankle stomp, ax hand to the throat or elbow strike to the base of the skull.

Role-playing attackers and victims are responsible to protect themselves at all times. Training with that assumption in mind assures an additional element of safety.

Absolutely the most dangerous partners are newbies because they don't understand how serious training injuries can be. They get amped up because they're doing something new and extreme. They're usually a little (or a lot) intimidated at first. They haven't developed enough skill to control or balance their speed of execution with when or how to regulate power. They can't judge distance well enough to trust they won't get it wrong, and they don't know which techniques are safe to throw hard and land on a training partner. Finally, they don't know when to pull power from a technique or which techniques should be practiced at full power *near* the target but not *on* it.

Hell, new students can even be dangerous when striking pads. Without the skill or control to fire off full-power elbow strikes and keep them on the pad, they're bound to skip one off and smack their training partner in the face.

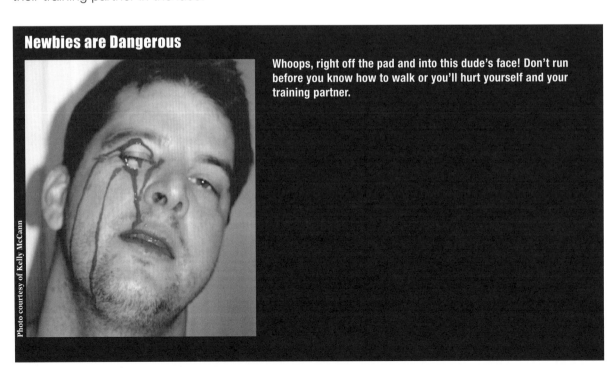

Newbies are Dangerous

Whoops, right off the pad and into this dude's face! Don't run before you know how to walk or you'll hurt yourself and your training partner.

Photo courtesy of Kelly McCann

We have a saying in firearms training: "Go slow to go fast." That means you have to fully understand and be competent in executing all the fundamentals of tactical shooting before you can push your personal limits of speed and accuracy. Similarly, if you're patient in combatives training, you'll develop skill quickly. You'll ultimately become far more effective and dangerous if you just remember to walk before you try running. Give your skills a chance to catch up to your enthusiasm.

A PROPER MIND-SET

Setting and achieving training goals is important to measure your improvements and maintain the quality of your training. With training time as limited as it is, it's essential to ensure you train as efficiently as possible. You'll have a lot of goals, but one of the most important to develop as you train is a proper mind-set.

Mind Over Matter (I Don't Mind and It Doesn't Matter)

Photo by Suzanne Carr Rossi

1. I'm using a closed ASP baton to put Jack in some pain as he sinks a rear naked choke on me. How hard am I grinding it in? As hard as my mind-set enables me to go.

2. By the way, caught in a situation like this on the street, you could draw your folding knife and either use it closed in the same way as the training scenario to create pain. You could also open it and cut your way out of the choke if you thought the attacker was going to choke you to death.

In the first picture in the above sequence, Jack's got the proper training mind-set. He's not cutting me any slack. He's really trying to pull me all the way back, push his hips up and choke me out. If I've got the proper training mind-set, I'll counter as hard as I have to in order to make him unwilling to hang on any longer. Anything less from either of us and I wouldn't trust this technique to work on the street.

The bottom line is you want to train with the same mind-set you'll have fighting for your life on the street. You're not using all your power but you're still using enough against a committed training partner to get honest reactions and results.

Visualization is also critical for accessing the same emotions you'll feel under the duress of a real attack. While you're training, remind yourself constantly that you're striking an actual attacker and not your training partner or a pad. When knife training, cover and fend visualizing a live blade in your partner's hand.

HEIGHTENED AGGRESSIVENESS

Another important training goal is heightened aggressiveness. You want to shove, jerk, pull and unbalance your training partner. Attack with your whole body and not just the limb you're using for the strike. Constantly think:, "He's standing where I want to be." Then forcefully take his space from him over and over again. Your partner benefits from your heightened aggressiveness because, even though you're only training, he actually *has* to protect himself.

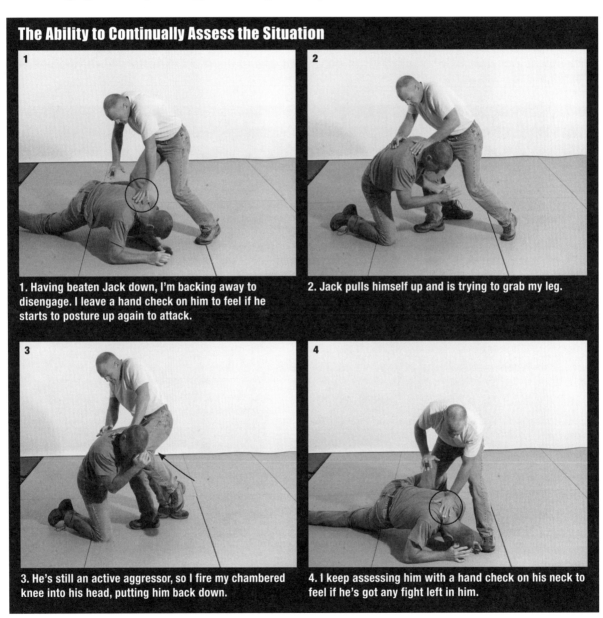

The Ability to Continually Assess the Situation

1. Having beaten Jack down, I'm backing away to disengage. I leave a hand check on him to feel if he starts to posture up again to attack.

2. Jack pulls himself up and is trying to grab my leg.

3. He's still an active aggressor, so I fire my chambered knee into his head, putting him back down.

4. I keep assessing him with a hand check on his neck to feel if he's got any fight left in him.

I've discussed the need to continually assess your situation throughout the book. Because you are in a heightened-aggressive state in a street fight, you've got to continually assess your attacker's condition as you beat him down in order to regulate your own use of force, keeping you from going over the top. Another reason to continually assess your situation is so you can feel what your attacker's doing as early as possible, enabling you to use your heightened aggression to prevent it and finish him—ultimately stopping him from prolonging the fight.

In training, heightened aggression and assessment skills develop your "fighter's eye," enabling you to see and understand your training partner's reactions and movements. Use your sense of touch by constantly "checking" him with your offhand, leg or the back of your forearm in order to feel his reactions and movements. Exploit any openings or opportunities as quickly as they occur. Never lose contact with your training partner (or an attacker) once you've risked closing on him.

Remember, fighting is all about risking *being* hurt in order *to* hurt. Once you've gained ground by taking an attacker's space, don't give it back. Take anything that's left.

INITIALLY ADAPTING TO YOUR ATTACKER, THEN MAKING HIM ADAPT TO YOU

Initially adapting to your attacker means you almost instantly understand what the important elements of an attack are, recognize what isn't important and use the fastest technique to mitigate the threat.

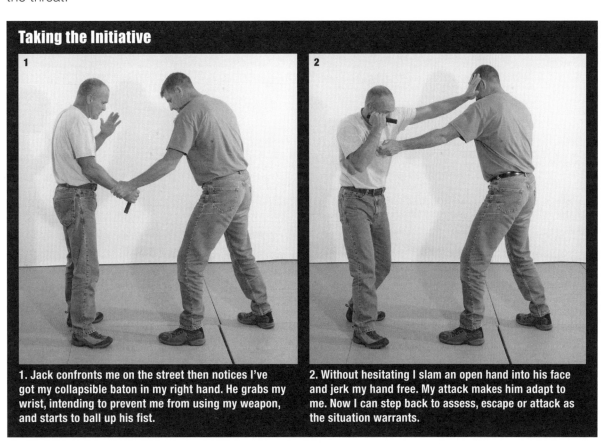

Taking the Initiative

1. Jack confronts me on the street then notices I've got my collapsible baton in my right hand. He grabs my wrist, intending to prevent me from using my weapon, and starts to ball up his fist.

2. Without hesitating I slam an open hand into his face and jerk my hand free. My attack makes him adapt to me. Now I can step back to assess, escape or attack as the situation warrants.

In most martial arts, self-defense techniques teach you to react by focusing on the hand that grabs you then attempting to apply some type of wrist-manipulation technique. That's a dangerous approach. The hand that's grabbing you is the least of your worries; it's accounted for and can't hurt you. Worry about the attacker's *other* hand, what he has in it and what he's going to do with it; that's where the real danger is. Once you've initially adapted to him, you have to reverse the confrontational dynamic and make him adapt to you.

That's when you viciously take control of the situation. Your attacker isn't going to just hand control of the situation over to you, you've got to take it. That's why my best course of action in the sequence on page 75 was to ignore the hand Jack grabbed me with and immediately disrupt his attack by smacking his face or jabbing his eyes in order to break free. I'm mitigating the threat posed by the hand that's unaccounted for by attacking him, reversing the confrontational dynamic and making him adapt to me.

Encourage your training partner to be animated because any attacker on the street will be. Work on initially adapting your technique to his attacks in order to develop a spontaneous guard, as discussed in Chapter 5. Don't forget to change training partners often so you grow accustomed to different demeanors, abilities, sizes and levels of intensity. Make sure you work with both right- and left-handed partners.

BRANCHING (RAPID TARGET ACQUISITION)

Branching is seamlessly flowing from one technique to the next based on results as well as rapidly exploiting targets of opportunity as quickly as they appear.

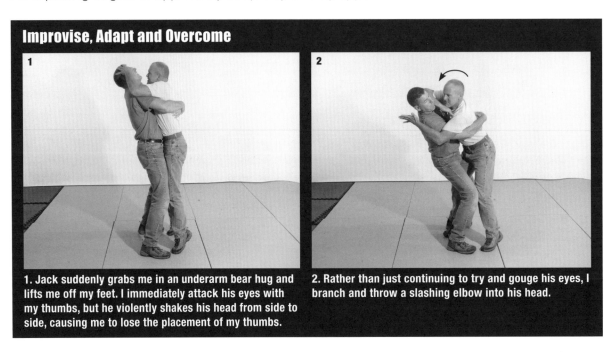

Improvise, Adapt and Overcome

1. Jack suddenly grabs me in an underarm bear hug and lifts me off my feet. I immediately attack his eyes with my thumbs, but he violently shakes his head from side to side, causing me to lose the placement of my thumbs.

2. Rather than just continuing to try and gouge his eyes, I branch and throw a slashing elbow into his head.

One of the most common mistakes in actual fights is not branching from a failed technique to a new one. Don't just get flustered when something you try fails or continue to attempt that same technique over and over until you succeed. Realize the futility in it. Stop struggling and try a new technique that may lead to finishing your attacker. When you're fighting for your life, you can't waste any time trying to get a failed technique to work.

Never underestimate an attacker's luck. While he's flailing away to save himself from you, he may see or feel an advantage too. He's probably an untrained fighter but he's very likely a survivor and skilled at making unexpected opportunities work to his advantage, which in effect is unskilled branching.

A characteristic of skilled combatants is how they continually throw different techniques at their attackers. If your technique had marginal or no effect at all it's unlikely to subsequently improve with another attempt. The momentary surprise associated with that technique and experienced by your attacker is gone. That's why you want to branch and continually make your attacker deal with new and different techniques. It's much harder for him to figure you out.

Branching from technique to technique is an essential skill in ground fighting because of continuous but fleeting opportunities. They're created by each fighter weighting and unweighting in order to achieve dominance and through sudden, explosive movements to gain an advantage.

You have to be vigilant in a ground fight because what appears to be a skilled ground fighter's sole focus may only be a distraction used to achieve better positioning or to disguise setting up a finishing technique. On the other hand, an unskilled thug can still create advantages for himself simply through instinctive scrambling.

In the following sequence, Jack and I grapple for dominance. It demonstrates how I branch techniques and how I use other combatives principles to achieve intermediate goals that lead to prevailing.

Branch, Branch and Branch Again

2. I reach across and replace my right hand with my left.

3. To keep him from posturing up, I continue to dig into his eyes and pull his head into my chest, trapping it with my left forearm. I lift my left shoulder up, *building a gap* to explode through and roll us in the reverse direction.

1. Jack shoots in for a two-leg takedown. I'm too slow to sprawl so I branch to another technique and grab his face, digging my fingers into his eyes. I *adapt to my attacker* having missed my opportunity to deny the two-leg takedown.

4. I jerk his head left and push it with my right hand. It's an explosive snapping action. I keep finger pressure in his eyes in the direction I want him to roll. He'll roll or his neck is toast; I *make him adapt to me.*

5. It works and I roll him. I *use my body weight*, push my chest into his face while staying close and making him unable to scramble free.

6. I use the opportunity to *incidentally strike* him, slamming both my hands down onto his head. This keeps his noggin flat on the ground and prevents him from looking at me. At this point he's getting beat up, physically and mentally. I'm breaking his will.

Continued ➡

7. I take my hands off his head to fire off a *full body-weight slashing elbow*.

8. Ouch!

9. Jack rolls over in an attempt to protect himself from more elbows and gives me his back but he buries his chin to defend against a choke. I go to his eyes to lift his head. If you've been paying attention you'll recognize that *I'm creating pain to create space* which is the opening I need to sink a choke.

10. G'night, Jack.

It took a long time to write the photo captions explaining the whole sequence so you'd be aware of everything going on. It probably took awhile to read it and look at the corresponding photos. Make sure you understand from the time Jack got my legs, the whole thing actually took just seconds on the mat...

...because it will only take seconds on the street. The ability to branch quickly, picking up targets of opportunity as fast as they occur, can only be developed through intense training.

There's also a direct correlation between your training intensity and your intensity on the street. It's a safe bet every ground technique you'll use when you're tackled in the parking lot outside some gin mill you were just drinking in is going to be used at full power and executed by snapping, jerking or yanking. Your training has to prepare you for that.

If you have branching skills and realize you're losing and may be seriously injured or killed, you'll successfully branch away from unarmed techniques in time to draw a weapon and use it in self-defense. A well-rounded street-oriented curriculum prepares you for this, teaching you to draw weapons—like pistols, knives, collapsible batons or using an improvised weapon—under duress to use in order to prevail in life-threatening situations.

CONSISTENT STRONG FINISHES

Whenever a student is unhappy with how he executed a technique, it's not uncommon for him to interrupt the move, ask a question, express his dissatisfaction or finish it in a half-assed way out of frustration. It's one of the worst habits students develop if they're not corrected. IT'S NOT OVER UNTIL IT'S OVER. On the street, you'd never stop pressing your attack if your ax hand wasn't up to par or your shin kick missed, so don't stop in training.

Remember the example of my friend at the end of Part I? Having fatally stabbed one attacker, he threw an ineffective ax hand at the second who had gotten the angle on him. Rather than being frustrated, he remained situationally aware, assessing the situation. He saw the attacker bend over to pick up his partner's dropped knife and seized the opportunity to drive his knee into the criminal's ribs. This not only hurt the criminal, it knocked him away from the knife. Staying in the fight mentally and looking for a strong finish may have saved my buddy's life.

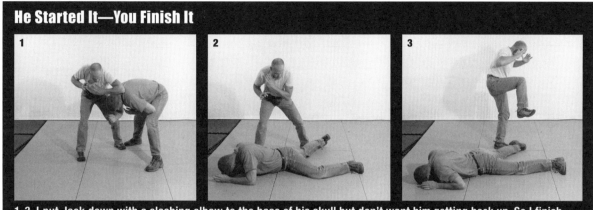

He Started It—You Finish It

1-3. I put Jack down with a slashing elbow to the base of his skull but don't want him getting back up. So I finish him with an ankle stomp. If you don't finish strong, you're potentially allowing the attacker another opportunity to prolong the fight. End it as quickly and resolutely as possible.

Whether you're training or in an actual self-defense situation, every strike ends with another chambered weapon ready to strike. Every sequence ends only when you achieve a better, more tactically advantageous position and are ready to strike again—or it doesn't end.

I've pointed out the reasons for this before. There's no consistently reliable result when you're fighting. You've always got to be chambered until you're clear of imminent danger. It's not over until it is.

In order to reach these training goals, combatives training has to be systematic. Time spent organizing your training regimen ensures that you practice each physical task, apply the combatives principles I've discussed and attain all your training goals.

ORGANIZING COMBATIVES TRAINING

For the firehouse fight club I described in the preface, I easily organized training by creating 5-by-7-inch index cards, each of which had the complete night's workout. We used to bang for three hours. One hour was dedicated to unarmed fighting, another to stick, and the last to knife fighting with a 10- to 15-minute break in between each. Each card had enough material to keep everyone busy for three hours.

We'd dedicate a fourth hour to camaraderie—drinking a beer or two with each other. Sometimes we'd watch instructional videos from other styles or discuss ideas about training or improvising training gear. Sometimes we'd just drink beer and bust each other's balls—women included.

A training schedule of one session a week is plenty. If you can handle more than that, you're not banging hard enough. About the time your soreness goes away and you've healed from the last training session, it's time for the next. I recommend you create 12 cards that cover three months of training. Rearrange and recycle the cards every 90 days. When you begin a new year, develop 12 totally new cards.

Here's an example of a couple workout cards:

Monday #8

Unarmed	Stick	Knife
Warm-up	**Strikes**	**Cuts & Stabs**
Medicine Ball	angles	slashing angles
Tumbling	blocks	thrusting angles
Flow & Fend	block & strike	
Strikes 5 (r) 5 (l)		blade blocks
	Sequences	block & thrust
Sequences		
	redondo	**Sequences**
(r) spearing elbow	recovery	
(r) axe hand	face mash	draw
neck down	hook kick	open #2 slash
(r) knee x2		#5 thrust
(l) slashing elbow	closed ASP	face mash
	take-down	
(l) eye jab		guard
(r) straight knee	closed ASP	#1 thrust
(r) hammerfist	grabbing attacks	chin rip take-down
		ankle stomp
Self Offense Scenarios	**Drills**	
		Drills
2 handed wall choke	T-Ball Bat	
rear overarm bearhug	O strike & block	snap cut speed drills
(r) (l) lapel grab	high - low	
		guard - fend - draw -
Ground Fighting		attack
deny the mount		
mount reversals		
guard release		
mount to arm break		
sequence		

Monday #11

Unarmed	Stick	Knife
Warm-up	duress draws to guard	closed knife pain compliance
Strikes 5 (r) 5 (l)	2 handed power strikes	closed knife grabbing attacks
3 strike speed drill		
Box Drills		closed knife striking sequences
Counter-Weapons	**Sequences**	
pistol head (f)	Styers' sequence	**Drills**
pistol chest(f)	Fairbairn sequence	
pistol back		(outdoors b/w cars)
	closed ASP striking sequence	touch n' go
stick #2		forearm choke cut-out
stick #3	**Drills**	
		Freestyle
box cutter attack	full contact sparring	
confined knife attack		
Self Offense Scenarios		
side headlock		
guillotine		
standing, rear arm choke		
Ground Fighting		
cover, clear, draw & stab		
mounted finger choke		
standing guard to mount		
countering the buck		

Make sure all the techniques in your curriculum are reflected in the cards you create, so for each three-month period, you know you've covered the whole curriculum. It's up to you how long within each hour you dwell on particular drills, strikes, scenarios or sequences. More often than not, I'd get everything accomplished on the card. But sometimes I wouldn't be able to complete the card if we had new people or if the usual crew was having trouble with a particular skill.

I also created some "wild cards." A wild card contains an out-of-the-box drill that might include unarmed, stick or knife techniques or a combination of them. For example, a wild-card scenario might start off as an unarmed attack and then escalate into an edged-weapon attack. Shuffle the wild cards up. Let someone pick one at the beginning of the night and finish the night's training with it. Just set the scenario up where no one can see it and run each person through it cold so you maximize his or her unfamiliarity and increase the potential for startle.

Here are a couple of other ideas to keep the group fresh and develop their martial growth:

- host a guest instructor and let him teach some highlights from his curriculum
- set up a "scenario night" and rotate the group through four to six scenarios in a round-robin; each person should experience three iterations

Developing a well-organized training session is challenging but definitely results in more efficiency and enables a rapid-learning curve. Now that you're organized and have a systematic approach mapped out, let's discuss your conduct of training.

CONDUCT OF TRAINING

Conduct of training is military terminology for how to execute the training schedule. For example, what logistics, locations and equipment are involved as well as what tasks will be taught and how. The individual conduct of combatives training can accomplish meaningful improvements by focusing on power development, combative movements and striking techniques. However, to develop your skills further depends on working with at least one training partner. Better still, you should train with a group so you can alternate partners and benefit from the energy that's created by people intensely training together.

Monkey See, Monkey Do

Photo by Suzanne Carr Rossi

If you get a group of newbies together with no previous skills, try learning by DVD. Gather the group around a laptop, choose a technique to watch and then duplicate it on the mat.

When learning from a DVD, briefly discuss the technique to ensure everyone knows what it ought to look like when they execute it. Identify the most important things to focus on—speed, power and balance for example. Break down into pairs and then practice. Keep repeating this process, referring to the DVD demonstration and practicing it until everyone's got it. Once everyone's fun meter is pegged on the technique, move on to another.

Something you'll find really helpful is setting up a video camera during training sessions. It doesn't matter whether your group is made up of all newbies, a mix of skill levels or very experienced practitioners because everyone will benefit from it. It's important everyone unequivocally see how they're doing instead of how they *think* they're doing.

After a number of repetitions of the technique, simply review the video comparing individual execution with the DVD demonstrations. There's nothing more efficient and productive than immediately fault checking performance and making instant corrections based on the video.

Similarly, instructors and students alike benefit when demonstrations of new techniques are conducted at full speed. After the full-speed demonstration, the technique should be broken down in detail and slowly explained. Then the technique should be demonstrated again at full speed. Any questions should be answered and followed by practice.

The reason this method is preferred is that, when new techniques are demonstrated slowly at first, it's human nature for people to mentally counter what they're seeing as it's explained. People don't necessarily understand the demonstration and the explanation took an artificially long period of time. On the other hand, when an unfamiliar technique is cooked off full speed, the group immediately sees its brutality and difficulty to defend against because they see it from an attacker's perspective, for the first time. He wouldn't know what's coming, and it's much more compelling.

Instructors should prowl the mat, making corrections and giving suggestions. They should encourage and mentor each student. Students participate in random demonstrations in order to experience what effective application feels like. The instructor's sheer intensity should be enough to transmit the message: There's no need for anyone to be brutalized.

Every so often normal training conditions should be intentionally upset. For example, the training environment should be made distracting or the actual training is made more difficult. The goal is to make everyone capable of achieving the same level of competence they're able to achieve under normal training conditions. Here are some ideas to accomplish what I'm talking about:

- Turn the overhead lights out and train in very dim light conditions.
- Turn the lights out and only use xenon white strobes set up at various angles.
- Turn some really terrible, bad, annoying music—or any sound recording like white noise for example—way, way up. You want it at the point you really can't stand it.
- When you're working on knife drills or any technique in which there's a real consequence for poor performance like hard blocking or fending, add some baby oil to everyone's forearms. The oil simulates the viscosity and slipperiness of blood. This makes it much, much more important (and much more difficult) to get blocks, fends and checks right.
- Train outdoors in the parking lot between each other's cars. (Training tip: Be careful of jeans with rivets. They'll tear up a car's paint job).
- Work your drills in confined spaces like stairwells or hallways. Use your head by training safely on lower stairs only.
- Get some old, overstuffed junk furniture and clutter up the training space. Train amidst it. Make each other deal with it.

The goal is to make students deal with every environmental condition and all types of attacks as intensely as the conditions you create allow. Training this way, no matter where or how they're attacked on the street, they'll have built up at least some level of familiarity with the situation.

Remember, in the first part of the book, I told you the only known way to completely negate the physiological effects of imminent danger was through experiencing frequent life threatening situations? I then explained how those would become the norm instead of the aberration?

Combatives training comes as close as you're likely to get. My students who've had violent encounters after they've trained with me have said they literally faced the attack thinking, "Shit, how much tougher than training can this be?"

Of course, the only thing you can't replicate is consequence, and that's the most important. It's what causes the most duress. Any student knows they shouldn't get stabbed, shot or killed in training. Still, depending on their appetite for intensity, you can come pretty close to duplicating the ferocity of a real fight for your life under fairly accurate conditions. Have at it, but ensure everyone's safety. In order to do that, you'll have to get some protective equipment and the right types of training aids.

TRAINING AIDS AND SAFETY

An essential element of injury prevention is your continuous exertion of common-sense control. Even with the proper equipment, you must *never* strike the throat, neck or base of the skull of your training partners with full power. You must *never* use a full-power chin jab on a training partner.

The gear described in this section will protect you from most pain and soft-tissue injury. It will NOT protect you from structural damage to the knees and ankles. For this reason, exercise caution when practicing low destructive kicks or angle/hook kicks to prevent serious injury to your training partner.

If you can afford to, buy law-enforcement defensive-tactics training equipment, otherwise known as DT training equipment. It's offered by manufacturers like RedMan, Blauer Tactical Systems or other alternatives. This gear is designed for heavy-duty organizational use and is preferable to most martial arts equipment. DT training equipment is well-made, purpose-built and typically offers better protection than martial arts equivalents. It's also much more expensive.

The protective equipment described in this chapter isn't used in accordance with the manufacturers intended use. This negates any liability of the manufacturer should it fail. I've used this equipment throughout the years with excellent results. Your decision to use the equipment as discussed in this book is a personal one. Combatives training is inherently dangerous and may result in serious injury or worse. Carefully consider your protective equipment before you use it. Inspect it often for signs of weakness, wear or indications it will fail. USE AT YOUR OWN RISK.

The equipment necessary to protect yourself "on the cheap" isn't expensive, exotic or difficult to find. You can improvise and make some yourself. But I recommend that you purchase durable equipment that'll last because combatives training focuses on developing powerful strikes. Nothing sucks more than having to interrupt a good training session because a piece of equipment blows out or unnecessarily injures someone. Source the right brand names by doing your research in combatives forums and asking experienced practitioners their opinions and preferences.

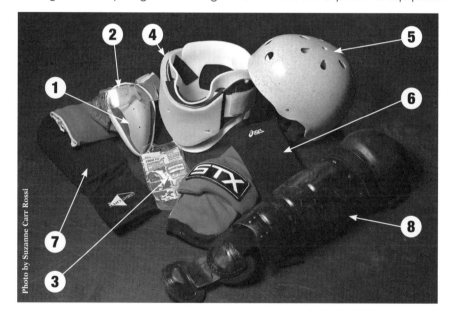

Photo by Suzanne Carr Rossi

What kind of equipment you wear depends on the drill you're working on. As you train harder, it'll become very apparent what gear to use during what drills and why. Trust me on that. Here's a list of essential personal equipment:

1. **Boat-style cup without athletic supporter.** Any cup you choose should be sturdily formed and provide complete coverage of your genitals. Remember you're not protecting yourself from the infrequent or unintentional groin shot in training. Instead, you're protecting yourself from focused and frequent groin attacks. If the edges aren't cushioned enough, add some small-diameter pipe insulation or bubble wrap. Wear the cup beneath your jeans without the athletic supporter.

2. **Racquetball glasses.** Your racquetball glasses should have molded in lenses and cushioning across your eyebrow ridges and the bridge and sides of the nose. Make sure they're well ventilated. You can modify some models by drilling holes along the sides, allowing more air to pass through and around your eyes to prevent fogging. Be sure you don't diminish frame strength or integrity by drilling too many holes or creating holes of a too-large diameter. You'll experience some pressure discomfort around the frames on impact—nothing you won't get used to. You still have to exercise care when you're training. The protection isn't 100 percent. While you're less likely to take a finger, training knife

or stick tip in the eye, weapons can still get behind the lenses. Some goggles provide adequate protection, but others won't sustain strong impact without the lenses popping out and potentially cutting the user. Whatever you choose should be sturdily built because you're protecting against focused, repetitive striking to the eyes and not unintentional or infrequent contact. If your training partner throws a face mash or finger jab too powerfully and his palm collapses, your glasses or goggles won't protect your nose.

3. **Comfortable mouth guard.** Choose a heat-moldable model. Take the extra time to ensure you've removed any seams left by the manufacturing process because exposed seams can irritate, abrade or cut the interior of your mouth. Fit it correctly, boiling it for the prescribed time. Make sure you suck the material up against the roof of your mouth so it stays locked in place.

4. **Cervical collar(s).** Blocking then immediately striking the neck is consistently used in combatives. Using cervical collars allows you to actually strike the side of your training partner's neck, but you still can't use full power. I use a hard cervical collar (Miami J) that's wrapped in an additional foam cervical collar. It limits the articulation of the training partner's head, provides stability and reduces the whipping rotational and angular motion of the head. It also protects the sides of the neck and larynx and the hand of whoever's striking. A plastic cervical collar can crack or break resulting in cuts. They may also collapse from external pressure and/or force. Do not strike cervical collars with full power.

5 **Pro-Tec style helmet** These are great for protecting the base of the skull in conjunction with the cervical collar. Make sure you get a full helmet and not a half helmet. These are available at outdoor adventure stores and are used for kayaking, whitewater rafting, climbing and other sports.

6. **Lacrosse arm pads.** These are terrific for both knife and stick training. You can choose the soft style or those incorporating hard protection at the elbow and lower forearm. Sized correctly, they provide coverage from the lower forearm up to and including the triceps. Sweeeeeet!

7. **Forearm and bicep pads.** Lacrosse pads protect the outside of the arm, but these protect the inside when worn spun around. Your forearm, stick or training knife forcefully impacts the inside of your training partner's arm when he attacks. These pads reduce trauma to soft tissue, but you and your training partner should still expect to get bruises.

8. **Baseball catcher's shin guards.** These provide excellent impact protection from shin kicks but, because they're not braces, shin guards will *not* prevent hyperextensions or injuries from lateral force on the knee and ankle. Your training partner should stay light on the leg being kicked and maintain a slightly bent knee, absorbing the force by letting his leg swing away on impact.

Two other pieces of equipment that are useful but not pictured here are:

• **Muay Thai thigh pads.** These are specifically designed to protect yourself when your training partner is practicing full-power angle kicks. Using them allows him to develop his speed, power, hip rotation and lead-foot pivoting. They don't protect your knee against his angle/hook kick.

- **Chest protector.** The spearing elbow is another staple in combatives and is an exceptionally powerful and painful technique. A quality chest protector prevents injury and enables your training partner to blast in using max violence of action. Chest protectors vary greatly in coverage area, foam density and the integrity of the cover material. Make sure you get one that provides maximum frontal density as the spearing elbow targets center mass.

STRIKING PADS, TRAINING AIDS AND IMPLEMENTS

Higher quality striking pads last longer and typically have better foam cores. They're less likely to "sack" after repeated, powerful striking. Sacking occurs when the impact protection thins out at the point of impact or is pushed toward the outside of the pad, away from where it's needed most. You'll know a pad is shot when you can feel the bone of your training partner's shins, ulna or hand through the pad.

The same is true of kicking shields and selecting the most durable covering is important because you'll train in street shoes and boots. Choose ballistic nylon over vinyl because it won't "grab" your foot like rubberized pad covering, potentially creating a tripping hazard. It also lasts longer than vinyl.

1. Muay Thai curved forearm shields. These are great for hand strikes—hammerfists, ax hands, cupped-hand blows, etc.—and for slashing elbows. Don't buy pads that are small, square shaped and have no curvature because they wobble on impact.

2. Kicking shields. Buy the slightly curved ones. The foam core should be dense but not too stiff. If the core is too stiff, the pad will "wobble" off your training partner's thighs and shins when kicked or kneed hard. Handle placement is equally important. Choose pads that incorporate at least three straps—two running longitudinally and at least one laterally. When the cover material tears and rips, have the shields reupholstered with upgraded cover material.

3. Muay Thai banana bag. Get a long one that's prewrapped and not filled. The difference is that wrapped material won't settle over time with use. Filler material compacts and eventually makes the bag too hard and painful to work out on. KO Thai Bags, like those found at www.kofightgear. com, provide just enough resistance but are completely satisfying to kick hard. Hang your bag so you can move 180 degrees around it, throwing left and right kicks, hand strikes and

Photo by Suzanne Carr Rossi

elbows at will. The bag should be high enough that you can strike it with your elbows in fully articulated arcs.

4. **Grappling dummy.** These are particularly useful in combatives training because they serve double duty when placed upright in a corner for kicks, hand strikes, knees, elbows and weapons or when laid down for ground and pound. There are many styles of grappling dummies to choose from; some are better than others. Pick one at least one third of your own body weight. Two arms should protrude for knife and stick targeting as well as "clearing" drills in stand-up practice. If you choose one with two legs, you can more accurately practice your groin attacks. Dummies are well suited for combatives because you can also trip and throw them. They're not cheap but do give you big bang for your buck.

IMPROVISED TRAINING EQUIPMENT

Let your imagination run wild. Part of what's admirable about combatives is the ingenuity used by people to get their training done in the most cost-efficient or expedient manner.

There are lots of ways your can improvise. I've used spare tires (wheel and tire) lag bolted to 6-by-6 decking supports for stick targets. I've also used ballistic rubber blocks glued to walls for live-blade practice. I've filled or stuffed all kinds of cotton duck, canvas or ballistic nylon bags with various materials for striking. And I've sourced wrestling-mat remnants to use on vertical surfaces for wall techniques or for wrapping supports used as striking targets—poles, beams, etc.

Start out by testing your creations with greatly reduced power. Slowly build up power and intensity, and check frequently for signs of weakness or failure in your design. You need to be confident what you've built will hold up against full power and won't break, creating hazards or any unsafe conditions.

FACSIMILE WEAPONS

Using training weapons that accurately represent real-weapon attributes is incredibly important. Pistols don't bend so throw away the cheesy rubber jobs. Knives don't bend either so junk the knock-off rubber tantos you got from the martial arts warehouse super blowout last year.

Buy or make your own implements out of wood or a Delrin cutting board. Chamfer all edges of the weapons, and sand the wood completely to prevent splintering. All you really need to work with these materials is a hacksaw, a Dremel tool, a rough-bastard file and 200- to 400-grit sandpaper.

Make sure the point of any training knife is completely rounded and unable to penetrate skin.

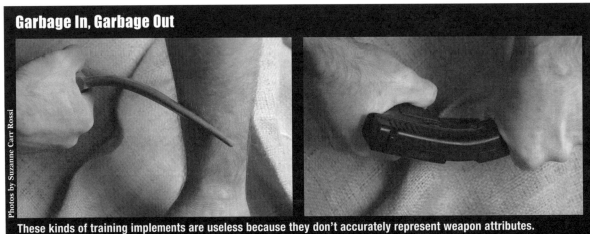

Garbage In, Garbage Out

Photos by Suzanne Carr Rossi

These kinds of training implements are useless because they don't accurately represent weapon attributes.

You can fabricate balls onto the rounded tips out of epoxy or J-B Weld. Round all edges enough to guarantee they can't break skin when slashing or stabbing. Wrap Vet Wrap around the grips of training pistols, knives or sticks to improve grip, or use a piece of bicycle inner tube stretched over the grip.

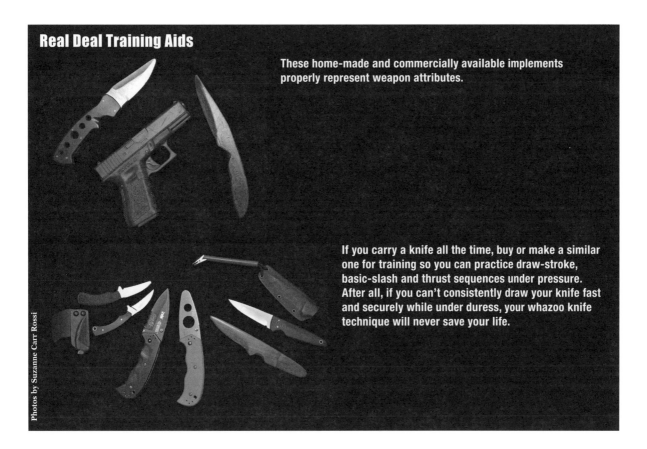

Real Deal Training Aids

These home-made and commercially available implements properly represent weapon attributes.

If you carry a knife all the time, buy or make a similar one for training so you can practice draw-stroke, basic-slash and thrust sequences under pressure. After all, if you can't consistently draw your knife fast and securely while under duress, your whazoo knife technique will never save your life.

Photos by Suzanne Carr Rossi

If you make your own training pistols—from wood or Delrin—leave the trigger guard off. They trap fingers. When the pistol's wrenched away during counter-weapon drills, fingers can be broken. Also leave the sights off; they cut divots out of skin and lacerate foreheads and faces when the pistols are knocked from someone's hands unexpectedly.

Some people buy Delrin training sticks for stick training. Although they're about as indestructible as you can get, they transmit shock down the shaft and directly into the hands when stick meets stick. After a couple hours training, you'll have numb, achy hands. Using sticks made of the harder woods like oak, hickory, maple and cocobolo produces the same pain and may also chip, creating eye hazards.

I like ⅞-inch diameter and 22-inch long rattan sticks. Forget the decorations, the burned or carved patterns and all that crap. If you're in love with the way a stick looks, you're not going to knock the shit out of it. Don't wrap it, dink with it or do anything but swing it.

Ratty Old Rattan

Good rattan "husks" with hard use. It will not chip, crack or simply snap. When you get cooking with a partner, you can actually smell the rattan burning and see wisps of smoke—how cool is that?!

Photo by Suzanne Carr Rossi

If you're not up to full-contact training with rattan sticks, make some full-contact training sticks. Buy some ¾-inch PVC pipe and black rubberized pipe insulation. Cut the PVC pipe to size and round both ends. Using 3M spray adhesive, spray both the pipe and the inside of the pipe insulation. Let dry. *Carefully* position the pipe insulation around the pipe and press it on. It behaves like contact cement so take your time. Once the two surfaces meet, that's it.

Improvised Training Stick

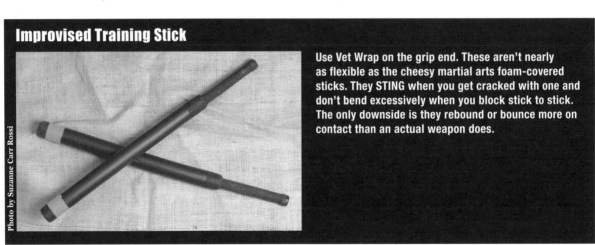

Use Vet Wrap on the grip end. These aren't nearly as flexible as the cheesy martial arts foam-covered sticks. They STING when you get cracked with one and don't bend excessively when you block stick to stick. The only downside is they rebound or bounce more on contact than an actual weapon does.

Photo by Suzanne Carr Rossi

The good news is you can go pretty damned hard with these improvised training sticks—bruising and welting each other up without real injury. If you catch a strike on the bones that form the orbits of the eye it may split the skin. The skin lays on top of bone there without much cushion, so wear your eye protection. The upside is, if it happens once, you're unlikely to let it happen ever again.

But because things like that *do* happen on occasion, it's important to know a little first aid and to stock up on first-aid items. You'll need them frequently during training.

FIRST AID

Inevitably, you'll suffer some training injuries. Remember I told you about the irreverent T-shirts? One year, I put "My Lifestyle Hurts" on the front of our shirts. On the back was a longitudinally-oriented, huge orange caplet (an 800mg Motrin) with the caption, "Motrin is my friend."

My opinion is that it's good to be sore after a hard workout. It's good to have some deep-tissue bruising and to know you can handle some pain and endure it. It's also a pleasant reminder that

Photo by Suzanne Carr Rossi

Remember to spray any shared equipment (especially headgear or anything contacting the skin directly) with a weakened solution of water and bleach to preclude "staph" infection (Staphylococcus aureus) from developing.

somewhere, the poor bastard who may attack you is NOT training nearly as hard as you—if at all.

Having a basic knowledge of first aid is just smart if you're training hard. Knowing when to suck it up and when to go see the doc is important. It may be the difference between being able to continue training or having to sit out a week because you didn't.

Similarly, it's everyone's personal responsibility to practice good hygiene. You don't want to sling snot and spit everywhere or release blood-borne pathogens all over the training venue and each other. It's everyone's responsibility to not spread the flu or the common cold to their training partners. If you're sick, DON'T COME TO TRAINING.

Frequent hand washing is a must because your hands are in each other's faces all the time. Clean, properly groomed fingernails are also mandatory. It's your responsibility to take anyone aside who needs to be told—as awkward as that may be—to clean their raggedy ass up before they come to training. Sounds odd you'd have to address something so basic, but I've certainly been surprised by some people's lack of personal hygiene. Besides the price of not handling hygiene issues is sickness—NOT cool.

Make sure everyone removes anything sharp from their body that might injure a training partner, including clip-on folders, watches, belt buckles, boots with sharp and bent-up eyelets, etc.

Here are a few things you can throw into your first-aid kit that are so useful you'll find yourself having to replenish them constantly:

1. **Band-Aids!!!** Love 'em, all kinds—knuckle, fingertip, with Neosporin and without, active strip ones, clear waterproof bandages…I FREAKIN' LOVE BAND-AIDS!!!!

2. **Liquid bandage products.** All kinds of different choices exist. Some stop the bleeding, some don't. You can use this stuff to hold down small flaps of skin or to coat split fingertips and cover shallow lacerations. The best stuff is used by your doctor and called Dermabond. It's a topical

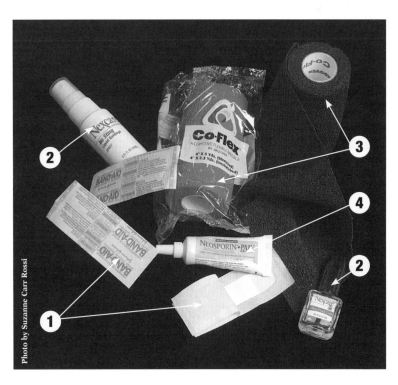

Photo by Suzanne Carr Rossi

cyanoacrylate adhesive or like skin Super Glue. It's particularly useful for injuries related to contact sports when the skin has been split from impact.

3. **Co-Flex.** A rubberized gauzelike material that provides a waterproof wrap that sticks to itself not to your skin. It's useful for binding two fingers together in the event you suffer a sprained or dislocated finger. It's also useful for affixing a sterile gauze dressing against a wound after cleaning it and applying a topical antibiotic.

    You can also save yourself a bunch of money and visit any equestrian or pet store to buy Vet Wrap. It's essentially the same stuff as Co-Flex but isn't sterile, so don't put it against an open wound without covering the wound first. AND it comes in a gazillion colors from fluorescent pink to black. In fact, I'm wearing some on a broken knuckle in the photos throughout this book!

4. **Neosporin!** Hoo-Ray! NOTHING worse than a suppurating wound! Neosporin contains three—count 'em THREE—antibiotics AND an external analgesic for pain. Remember to clean the wound, coat it and cover it. This is where those cool Band-Aid bandages that have Neosporin already in them work great because they're expedient. Simply wash the wound and slap one on—done!

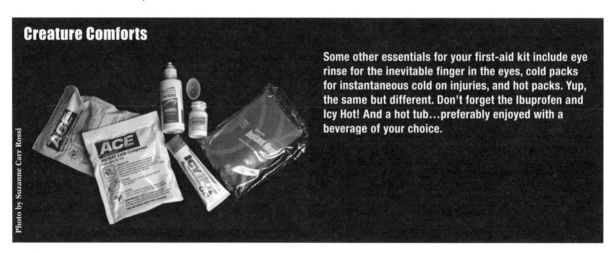

Creature Comforts

Photo by Suzanne Carr Rossi

Some other essentials for your first-aid kit include eye rinse for the inevitable finger in the eyes, cold packs for instantaneous cold on injuries, and hot packs. Yup, the same but different. Don't forget the Ibuprofen and Icy Hot! And a hot tub...preferably enjoyed with a beverage of your choice.

NOTE: NEVER coat and cover a suppurating wound before cleaning. DO NOT clean the wound in the hot tub *or* the beverage of your choice. Do NOT wear your cold pack into, or rinse your eyes in, the hot tub either.

CHAPTER 5
COMBATIVES POSITIONS AND MOVEMENTS

As you train, you'll become increasingly aware that combatives are actually a fusion of concepts, positions, movements, offensive and defensive postures, and striking techniques used in accordance with the principles you learned in Chapter 3.

It's important to understand this fusion before we move on. Without that context, you might mistake combatives as the stodgy, stiff and inflexible application of individual strikes. Nothing could be further from the truth. No single component of combatives is an end in itself. Each is used in conjunction with the others. You combine them to make you a more comprehensive and effective combatant.

By maximizing your fighting effectiveness, you avoid struggling. Remember, struggling only saps your energy and distracts you from finishing. Struggling isn't prevailing or losing. It's combatives purgatory—limbo. Once you successfully fuse all the components of combatives, you'll be fighting at the pinnacle of efficiency and will consequently struggle less and be capable of dominating your attacker far more quickly.

You've got to learn about all these components individually before you can fuse them together. As you read, just remember that they're mutually supporting and used simultaneously. For example, the guard position momentarily protects you so you can attack. You get out of your attacker's way by using an out-of-line movement in order to attack. You block to protect yourself *in a way* that enables you to instantly attack.

Listen, to be effective when you're fighting you have to constantly alternate between a defensive and an offensive posture and you continuously move, seeking to improve your position and marginalize your attacker's.

Those combined actions enable you to maintain a reasonably constant defense while you prepare to or actually attack.

A fight by its very nature is a struggle of opposing violent exertion made by you and your attacker in an attempt to dominate each other.

Photo by Suzanne Carr Rossi

Note: In order to implement combatives fusion in the text, I'm going to introduce some terms you're not yet familiar with in explanations. If I don't explain a term immediately that only means it's unnecessary at that moment. We'll get to it. Be patient.

Let's get started with combatives positions.

THE INDEX POSITION

An index position is nothing more than a stance you assume in any threatening, face-to-face situation you can't simply walk away from. You'll recognize when it's appropriate to "index" because you'll feel *really* uneasy and uncertain. Indexing enables you to instantly defend or attack without the appearance of being prepared to do either. Sweet! Two for one!

Indexing is like cocking a firearm. When you cock a firearm, you make it ready to fire, cutting the trigger pressure that you need to fire in half. When you index, you cock your own trigger by mentally committing to a pre-emptive attack in order to protect yourself if necessary.

To execute: Exactly how you index depends on what strike you're going to attack with. The index for an ax hand is not the same as the index for a chin jab. Incorporate whatever you devise as your "go to" index positions into your training by assuming one and then suddenly exploding and striking an impact pad as quickly and powerfully as you can. I've included some examples of particular index positions below. Use them as a template to build your own.

I usually default to a hands-up palms-out index position. (See page 112 for an example.) I move my hands ambiguously in an apparent effort to placate the thug or de-escalate the situation. I'm actually using the motion like a boxer to keep my arms loose and ready to strike. Even though I'm indexed, I've already visualized striking my attacker. He doesn't even realize that I've crossed the threshold of whether to attack or not before he has.

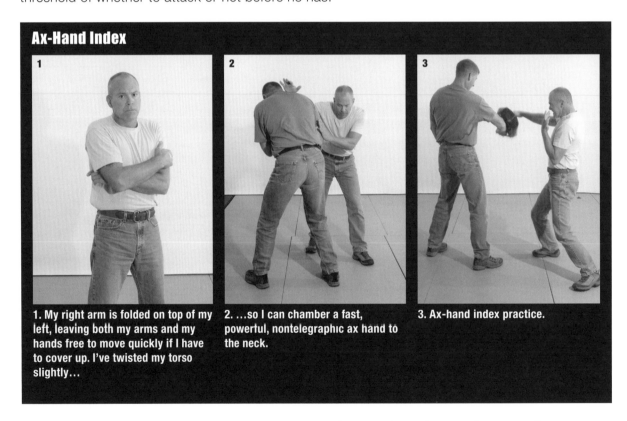

Ax-Hand Index

1. My right arm is folded on top of my left, leaving both my arms and my hands free to move quickly if I have to cover up. I've twisted my torso slightly...

2. ...so I can chamber a fast, powerful, nontelegraphic ax hand to the neck.

3. Ax-hand index practice.

Your index position is supposed to be conciliatory, but watch out for your face revealing your true intent or making you appear threatening. Don't give the bad guy a "hairy eyeball" by lowering your eyebrows and furrowing your brow. Lose the mean face. Just relax your jaw muscles and eyebrows or, even better, arch your eyebrows up and look hapless.

Chin to Chin Jab

1. I've got one forearm vertical and one horizontal passively covering my upper body in order to protect myself if necessary...

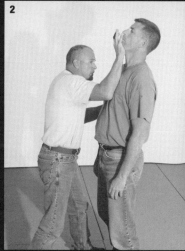

2. ...and support a nontelegraphic chin jab.

3. Chin to chin jab practice.

Index positions work because actions are always faster than reactions. If your hands are within reach of your attacker's face, there's nothing he can do to defend against your strike when you unexpectedly explode. Do you have any idea what a huge advantage that is and how much control that gives you over uncertain situations? When you index, it's not a foregone conclusion there's going to be violence. It only means there *may* be and you're prepared to pre-empt it.

Street Savvy

Jack confronts Marilyn and is threatening her. She indexes on him, getting both her hands up in a natural-appearing, nonthreatening way by appearing to hold her purse strap with one and showing Jack her other palm. She's set up to pre-emptively finger jab Jack's eyes with her left hand and run if she has to.

Photo by Suzanne Carr Rossi

Consider two different fighters in separate confrontations. One is street skilled and trained in combatives, the other is traditionally trained in the dojo. The street-skilled fighter tries to be avoidant but *will* unexpectedly attack his attacker because he's got an offensive mind-set. (Remember combatives principle No. 2.) On the other hand, the dojo-trained fighter has been taught to *defend.* He'll likely wait for his attacker to attack, giving up the significant advantage of action vs. reaction because he's got a *defensive* mind-set. Unfortunately, on the street, his choice may be fatal.

Think of it this way: Although both may hold their hands up to appease, combatives-boy has already mentally committed to *attacking*. Dojo-dude really is defending. Neither situation may result in violence, but if they did, combatives-boy would have the clear head start in his situation. Mentally, he's already victimized his attacker.

THE GUARD POSITION

Don't confuse the guard position with an index. The guard provides you protection if you're attacked and as you attack. The guard looks aggressive, but an index doesn't. When you assume the guard, it's because the confrontation has escalated, removing any doubt whether or not you're facing an attack. Depending on the situation, you may initially index on someone, strike him and then use the guard to close.

You don't ease into a guard. The "shit is on" as we say, which makes you "pop" into your guard as if you'd been touched with a lit cigarette whenever someone throws a strike, grabs you or spins you around. Your guard should become reflexive.

To execute: Tuck your chin slightly and raise your hands, keeping your elbows down and in front of your abdomen and ribs. Keep your head up and look through your hands at your attacker. Crouch slightly. Keep your feet offset and shoulder width apart.

Remember the axiom: "Nose over toes." Like so many other athletic stances, the guard position lowers your center of gravity and "centers" you, making it easier to quickly change direction to attack or defend, shift your weight and stay on balance.

If you're right handed, you're in the forward guard when your right foot is forward. When your left foot is forward, you're in the reverse guard. If you're a lefty, then it's the opposite; you're in the forward guard when your left foot is forward and reverse guard when your right foot is forward.

Standing Guard

1. Jack starts to throw a punch at me. I'm in a solid reverse guard and holding my hands high to protect my face and head. I keep Jack's head, hands, shoulders, elbows and hips in view, looking through my hands. I can freely articulate my arms and legs in order to defend against anything Jack throws.

2. This is a full frontal view of the reverse guard. I'm "nose over toes," I'm on balance and I can instantly move in any direction.

Choosing the forward or reverse guard depends on several factors. I usually default to a reverse guard because it's ingrained in me to keep my weapon side back and out of reach of a potential grab. Secondly, I learned to lead with my less powerful hand (an orthodox stance) because of my past training in boxing.

Tactically, the reverse guard does two things for you. First, it keeps your most powerful hand free if your attacker rushes you and ties up the first thing he runs into—your "weak" hand. Second, you can use your weaker hand for short-range attacks to his eyes and face, setting up your most powerful hand for frequent strikes and increasing the likelihood of a finishing opportunity.

You've got to risk being hurt in order to hurt, right? A good guard mitigates that risk because it isn't *defensive* even though it is a defense and provides you protection. Developing an intuitive guard enables you to instantly move in any direction, remain balanced and be prepared for anything, particularly to attack.

No matter what, whenever you're *not* moving in a fight, you should be in a well-balanced guard, slightly crouched with your feet shoulder width apart and offset, ready to explode into the attack. If your feet are too wide, too narrow or too parallel, correct the situation to be ready to rock. Now that you understand the guard position, let's broaden its application by adding movement.

COMBATIVES SHUFFLE

Because combatives is infighting, you'll constantly adjust your range to the attacker with movement. In boxing, infighters are also known as "pressure fighters" because they create and maintain constant pressure on their opponents. Infighters close explosively with their opponents and overwhelm them with furious flurries of punches. Combatives practitioners close explosively to overwhelm and finish their attackers with strikes and destructive kicks by any means necessary. When you're fighting, you'll constantly adjust your range with movement, perpetually seeking the advantage over your attacker.

The most basic combatives movement is the combatives shuffle. It's instantly familiar—recognizable in boxing, fencing, bayonet training and martial arts. Shuffling is simple and prevents you from ending a movement with your legs too wide and off-balance. It keeps you from crossing your legs, which makes you vulnerable to a shove, strike or tackle that could put you on your ass.

To execute: From the guard, simply lift your lead foot and propel yourself forward by pushing off your rear foot. When your lead foot lands, adjust your stance slightly by sliding your rear foot forward until your feet are shoulder width apart and offset again. Each shuffle is a two count movement—push-off and adjust. Say it to yourself as you learn.

To move rearward, step back slightly with your rear foot as you push off your lead. When your rear foot lands, adjust your stance by sliding your lead foot back until your feet are shoulder width apart and offset again. No matter which direction you move, repeat the process, adapting how you execute the shuffle to whichever direction you're moving.

Here's a hard one (kidding). Move backward on a left oblique from the reverse guard. Got it? Visualize where your feet are and the direction you're going to move. Okay, take a slight step to the rear with your lead foot as you push off your rear foot on a 45-degree angle in the same direction. Drop your lead foot even with your rear then slide your rear foot backward until it's shoulder width apart and offset again.

Now, move right rear oblique from the reverse guard. Think. Exactly! Take a slight step back with your rear foot on a 45-degree angle as you push off your lead in the same direction. Adjust with which foot? That's right, your left foot.

Depending on which guard you're in and what direction you're moving, shuffling incorrectly has different consequences. In the first example in which you moved left oblique and to the rear, stepping too deeply crosses your legs, which throws you off-balance, momentarily ties your legs up and makes you unnecessarily vulnerable to your attacker lunging. In the second example in which you moved right rear oblique, stepping too far overextends your legs, making them too wide to support a balanced guard position.

To learn shuffling, imagine you're standing in the center of a clock face. Now, shuffle twice forward to 12 o'clock then back to center. Next, shuffle twice backward to 6 o'clock then forward, returning to the center. Now shuffle to 3 o'clock and back, and now shuffle to 9 o'clock then back. Finish with oblique shuffles to 2, 10, 4 and 8 o'clocks.

Next, you link single shuffles in each direction. For example, shuffle forward once, backward once, then once right and left. Finish the drill by shuffling forward right oblique, forward left oblique, right rear then left rear.

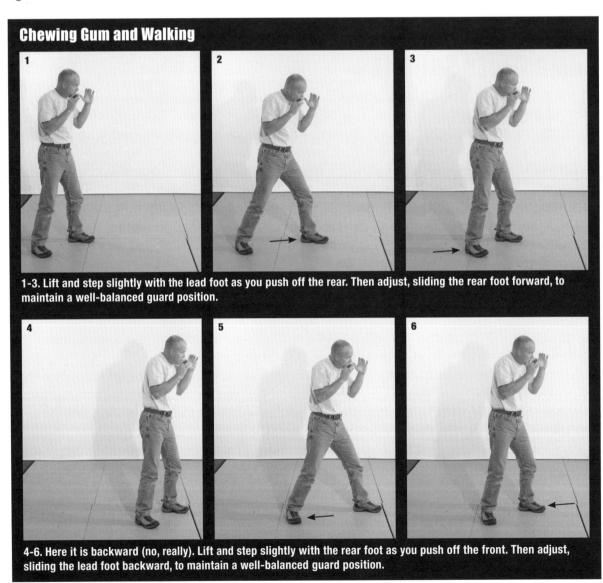

Chewing Gum and Walking

1-3. Lift and step slightly with the lead foot as you push off the rear. Then adjust, sliding the rear foot forward, to maintain a well-balanced guard position.

4-6. Here it is backward (no, really). Lift and step slightly with the rear foot as you push off the front. Then adjust, sliding the lead foot backward, to maintain a well-balanced guard position.

Have a Nice Trip. See You Next Fall.

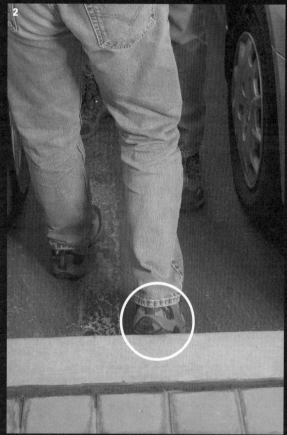

1. As Jack closes on me, I back away and my foot reaches its limit of advance. Trouble is, that with my heel flat, my foot stops, but my upper body continues backward, unbalancing me and perhaps making me stumble or fall.

2. (Please don't make me say moonwalk…!) Lifting your heel as you slide your foot back on the ball of your foot bends your leg at the knee. Consequently your heel is up if it unexpectedly runs into an obstacle leaving you on balance and able to deal with it without stumbling or falling down.

Even though I've used the word "step" in describing how to shuffle, don't confuse shuffling with merely stepping. Stepping doesn't connote forceful movement. When people step to walk, they pull as much weight behind them as they push forward. Think of walking as a relatively neutral movement. Each shuffle on the other hand is a forceful movement. You push your weight into whichever direction you're moving. Although shuffling is coordinated movement, it's certainly not graceful or dancelike. Combatives shuffling is using staccato bursts of energy to forcefully move.

VAULTING

Vaulting is nothing more than shuffling on steroids. You explode off your rear foot in the direction you're attacking, covering more distance more quickly and more forcefully than when you shuffle. Vaulting maximizes the power development formula I explained in combatives principle No. 9 on full body-weight striking, remember it?

When you vault you move more mass at a higher velocity over a greater distance to collide with your attacker weapon first. You crash through a gap using a vault in order to create a violent car crash. (Combatives principle No. 8.)

To execute: Apply what you learned about shuffling and just do it explosively. Have your training partner hold a kicking shield against his upper body while you assume the guard just outside of arm's reach to the shield. Now, explode off your rear foot and crash into the pad, knocking your training partner back. Rinse. Repeat.

Once you've got single vaults down, let's solidify the notion of closing repeatedly. Set up the drill the same way we just discussed but this time, when you knock your training partner back, *immediately* vault and crash into him a second time. Don't give him time to recover. The point of this drill is to repeatedly crash into him through the gaps you keep creating, making him increasingly unstable and unable to deal with it. Imagine the added effect when we start striking while we crash…Annihilation!

Every Journey Starts With a Step. Every Attack Starts With a VAULT!!!

Photos by Suzanne Carr Rossi

1. Jack starts to throw a right hand at my head. I've got a solid reverse guard.

2. I explode off my rear foot in his direction, making any adjustment to my guard as necessary to stay protected while I attack. In this photo, you can see my weight is being driven forward.

3. My body weight drops. I crash inside Jack's punch, making it inconsequential. I'm making my rear foot adjustment, bringing it forward to regain my…

4. …balanced guard position.

The purpose of the photos is to depict a vault. Jack wasn't wearing any protective equipment so I didn't bury my spearing elbow into his sternum. But these four photos should make you realize just how much force you're generating by fusing principles, movements and strikes. It's ugly.

Remember this simple axiom: "Stay on your toes and keep your attacker on his heels." It reminds you to constantly close on your attacker and why you should. He can't move backward fast enough to disengage from you when you repeatedly close on him by vaulting.

OUT-OF-LINE MOVEMENTS

Out-of-line movements are nothing more than pivoting to clear your body of an attack. They are tightly executed. Colloquially I call this "opening the gate." You're the gate. When an attacker lunges, you open the gate and let him though. Another analogy is a bullfighter. The bull charges, and at the last second, the bullfighter pivots out of the way. Now he's perpendicular to the bull and can attack while the bull is at a complete disadvantage.

To execute: Standing in a reverse guard, imagine someone lunging at you. Keep your hands up in a good guard, sweep your lead foot back in a tight arc, pivoting on the opposite foot. Snap your hip and shoulder back for speed. Recover in a balanced guard. Now you're perpendicular to your attacker's direction of attack.

Open the Gate

1. This is me standing in the reverse guard.

2. This is my completed out of line movement. Not too tough, eh?

To maximize training efficiency, have your training partner stand in front of you and just beyond arm's reach. Have him vault unexpectedly and directly at you. Open the gate and recover in a well-balanced guard.

Just like in bullfighting, moving out of line almost always presents an opportunity to strike. So if you have your training partner vault at you, you can slam the hand closest to him into his face as you open the gate. You're fusing these movements. Don't stand in front of him, slam your hand into his face and then open the gate. Similarly, don't open the gate and then, when you recover, slam your hand into his face. Combine these actions, moving out of line and slamming his face.

Let's add one more thing as a finish to the exercises in this section. Have your training partner vault directly at you, then open the gate and slam his face. The second you recover your guard, attack him again with a blindside vault. Repeat this drill over and over until your movements are deft, forceful and fast.

These fused movements—moving out of line then immediately attacking—disrupt your attacker, unbalancing him and putting him on the defensive. By the way, this is another great example of applying our combatives principles. You're avoiding offensively, clearing your body of the attack, relying on gross-motor movements, building and crashing a gap, using full body-weight striking and RAGING…with reason of course. That's six principles out of 14 in just one sequence of movements.

Bullfighting

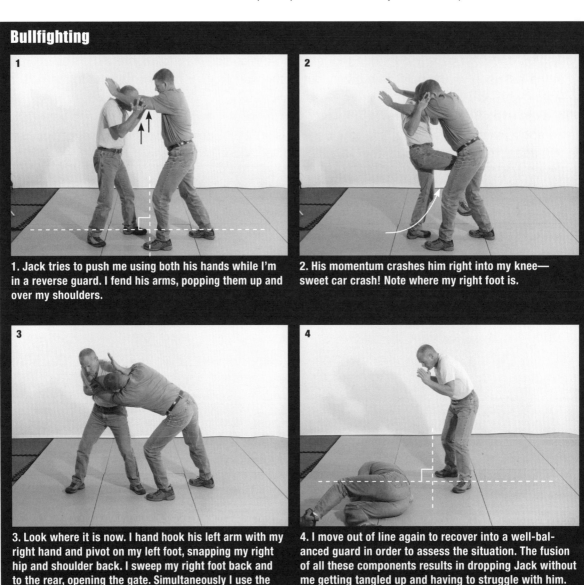

1. Jack tries to push me using both his hands while I'm in a reverse guard. I fend his arms, popping them up and over my shoulders.

2. His momentum crashes him right into my knee—sweet car crash! Note where my right foot is.

3. Look where it is now. I hand hook his left arm with my right hand and pivot on my left foot, snapping my right hip and shoulder back. I sweep my right foot back and to the rear, opening the gate. Simultaneously I use the leverage of that movement to drive my left ulna deep into Jack's right upper arm, hyperextending his elbow.

4. I move out of line again to recover into a well-balanced guard in order to assess the situation. The fusion of all these components results in dropping Jack without me getting tangled up and having to struggle with him.

When your attacker senses your movement, he may adjust his vector. By then you should be slamming your hand into his face or your fingers into his eyes. You can pivot tighter and faster than he can turn. Be prepared to partially sprawl as you move out of line because your attacker may go low in an attempt to get your legs and take you down. Open the gate decisively, and remember, you're only getting out of his way *in order to attack.*

As you accrue more training time, moving combatively becomes increasingly natural. You'll start to adapt it to all situations. In the example on the left, I'm using the exact same movement we just discussed to get out of my attacker's way, avoid a struggle, pull him off balance and maximize my striking power. Take a look.

SWAYING AND HOLLOWING OUT

Swaying and hollowing out are instinctive, quick combatives movements used to clear your body of a weapon's path. They're particularly useful (and occur naturally) when you're startled by a swing, stab or slash.

Situational awareness goes a long way toward minimizing your risk of being startled, but it can still happen. That's precisely when you'd either sway or hollow out, like when you just catch a glimpse of something flying at your head or gut. In these instances, it's everyone's instinct to jerk backward and out of the way.

Don't confuse swaying and hollowing out with perfectly planned and executed movements. To the contrary, they're both a "Hail Mary" 70-percent solution. You sway or hollow out out of urgency because there's simply no time to do anything else.

To execute: You sway with your upper body and you hollow out your midsection. Many times you'll have to link the two as reciprocal, consecutive movements because attackers frequently slash at your face then slash back low in the opposite direction to cut your gut. You've no doubt seen the novelty toy known as the Amazing Drinking Bird. It bends over and dips its beak into a glass then bobs its head back out of the glass. You get the picture.

Get into your guard facing and standing within arm's reach of your training partner. Wear your protective eye gear. Have him use a training knife and slash at your face. When you first begin, he should go slowly and then at increasing speeds and intensity as you master swaying.

Keep your hands up and sway back out of the path of the knife as if you'd been stung by a bee on your Adam's apple. Once you've got it down, have him slash high and immediately follow up with a reverse slash at your gut.

Describing how to hollow out is easy because it's such a familiar movement. You know how you push your butt WAY out when you're hugging Aunt Martha...all 300 pounds of her? You're like *wicked* careful to avoid full-body contact with her, right? Well imagine how fast you'd do it if she'd been in the bottle again and grabbed your ass to pull you in close. BAM! I'm thinking your speed of movement would break the sound barrier. Do that to clear your body of the slash aimed at your gut.

When you hollow out to avoid a gut attack, drop your hands slightly to concentrate your defense momentarily around your midsection. Articulate your elbows as necessary to protect your stomach. If you do get cut, it'll be on the back of your forearms instead of, well, you being eviscerated.

A Miss Is as Good as a Mile

1. I turn around just as Jack swings a club at my head—uncivilized bastard! I jerk and sway my upper body back out the way just in time.

2. Jack's just pugnacious. He menaces me, brandishing a knife. Then, he suddenly lunges at me, trying to stab my gut. I think he looks like Aunt Martha and save myself from being stabbed by thinking about hugging her last Christmas!

You've picked up on the simultaneity of combatives by now. In the example, I sway and hollow out to avoid injury but only because I have to in order to avoid anything that will take me out of the fight. But I can't keep doing that forever. After all, defending is just delaying an inevitable loss. You have to attack to prevail.

Left unhurt, your attacker will be emboldened and feel he can slash, hit or stab you without penalty. His attack will intensify. Although you have to protect yourself, you also have to make him doubt, make him regret, make him fear, remember? Here's how:

Not Self-Defense, Self-Offense

1. Jack slashes at my face with a backhand slash. As I sway back, I use my movement to shin kick his lead leg, hyperextending it. Nothing he tries to do to me comes without a price. I don't want him to feel he can freely attack without consequences.

2. I hollow out to avoid Jack's forehand slash at my gut, but as I do, I throw both my hands into his face, attacking his eyes to hurt him. I also disrupt his vision to make him think twice about continuing his attack.

Coordinated, explosive movements are fundamental imperatives in combatives. If you can't move well then you're at a disadvantage and, against a committed attacker, may end up helping him instead of hurting him. Spend some time developing your footwork, your explosiveness and your speed. Don't think of it as mundane. Think of it as time well spent learning to attack with your body.

The fusion of effective movement and powerful striking is frightening and should make even the baddest of asses a little nervous the second you cook off. Remember, the second your attacker thinks "Oh SHIT, what did I get myself into…?!" is the precise second you become the predator and he starts behaving like the loser he is.

CHAPTER 6
DEFENSIVE SKILLS

The guard position is the foundation for all combatives defensive skills. You've undoubtedly already realized the guard is effective because it incorporates full-body movement. You can get your whole body out of the way using an out-of-line movement or, as necessary, clear just your upper or midbody by swaying or hollowing out—all in your guard. Now let's incorporate hand skills that deflect grabs and strikes, making the movements you've already learned even more effective.

FENDING

When you were growing up, did you ever see some poor kid being bullied? Maybe he was backed up against a wall of lockers with his chin down behind one shoulder, hands up, hips twisted slightly away from the bully…huh. Sounds like the description of a pretty good guard. The bully, invading his victim's personal space, probably used twitchy feints to pretend he was going to throw a punch. The victim's reactions more than likely were overreactions that consequently opened him up to *really* be hit.

Weirdly, fending is similar to the bully's movements but defensive. You fend using the smallest hand-and-arm movements necessary to deflect or disrupt an attacker's strikes or grabs. Fending is intuitive but disciplined; you don't want to open up your guard by overreacting to a feint. Think of fending like flinching. It's combining upper-body, hand-and-arm and head movements as necessary to render an attacker's grabs or strikes ineffective.

To execute: Have your training partner stand within arm's reach. You want him to try and touch you anywhere from the waist up while alternating his hands. Assume your guard and use a combination of hand, arm and shoulder movements to deflect his reach. Keep your movements small; make them only as big as necessary to make his reach ineffective.

Amp your practice up by having your training partner put on some full-contact gloves to strike at you with medium power and speed. You'll incorporate upper-body and full-body movement. For example, use tight out-of-line movements, forward and reverse shuffles and swaying and hollowing out.

The fastest way to develop your fending skills is to force you to use them. Both of you need to put on your protective eyewear for this exercise. You'll back up against a wall. Rest your butt against the wall but keep your feet 24 inches or so away from it and lean forward from your waist up. Keep your hands up and elbows down. Look through your guard at your training partner. Have him use a training knife to slash and thrust at you while you use fending to deflect his attacks.

Finally, incorporate finger jabs and face mashes as stop-hits after a fend. Apply combatives principle No. 13, unarmed double taps, to make your stop-hit strikes indefensible. Keep your power under control and build speed and intensity as your skill improves.

Can't Touch This

1. I'm backed up against a wall, and Jack's trying to grab me with his right hand. From my guard, I move my upper body slightly in the opposite direction and move my left hand and arm slightly to fend his reach.

2. He follows up with a left hand hammerfist. I move my upper body in the opposite direction and fend by raising my right elbow while covering my head and face.

3. Jack follows up with a low right hook to my body. I hollow out and drop my elbows to protect my ribs and abdomen.

4. He follows up with a left-hand stiff arm to my face. I sway back, lift my hands to fend and twist away.

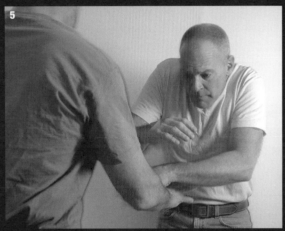

5. Jack shoots his right hand at my gut. I hollow out and collapse my forearms down onto his to fend it. My right arm is prepared to defend against a follow-up left hand shot from him.

So what's the point of all this? Remember our hypothetical example with the bully earlier? What if the kid being tormented had read this book and built up his skills? When the bully blocked his path, he wouldn't freak. Instead he'd index and visualize smacking his tormentor. If the bully feinted by flicking a hand at his face, our guy wouldn't overreact. He'd pop into his guard and fend only to suddenly explode with a face mash. The bully, caught totally off guard, would land on his ass and wonder what just happened when—POW! He gets a knee in his face from his intended victim. OUCH!

The bully loses and lives in shame for the rest of his life. Our boy gets the girl, an iPod phone, a cool car and is the BMOC (big man on campus)—*very* cool. See? This book is life altering!

I hope that you're understanding fending is an essential skill. The following excerpt is from a letter sent to me by Chuck D. After learning fending from some of my instructional DVDs, he was brutally attacked in September of '02 by a thug who was wielding a carpet cutting knife:

Dear Mr. McCann,

Coming out of a park and back onto the main street, I saw a young guy walking toward me. As we passed each other, he slammed his shoulder into mine spinning me around. He was a big guy, over 6 feet and 200 pounds. As I spun around so did he. His arm was already in the air and slashing down at me. No words. No looks. No NOTHING! Just violence like I've never experienced before. I was able to fend my attacker off, getting to the inside of a few of his slashes (just like you demonstrated in tape #3).

I remember watching you and the other guy work basic slashes and I was amazed as this "full bore" slash just bounced off of your fend position like hail bouncing off a rooftop. Not only did your fends protect you from the assault, but I also noticed that it made it very difficult for the attacker to realign himself to set up for another assault. I began making fending part of my everyday workout. I drilled it everyday. Worked it as a startle technique.

So when I was attacked, the first thing I did was fend!! I didn't even think about it.

The incident ended when Chuck created an opportunity to finish by using an angle/hook kick to break his attacker's base, putting the man down on the ground. He kicked the thug in the head then ran from the scene. He sustained only the gash shown in the photo below. Funnily enough, despite having a clip-on folding knife with him, there simply wasn't time for Chuck to draw and use it.

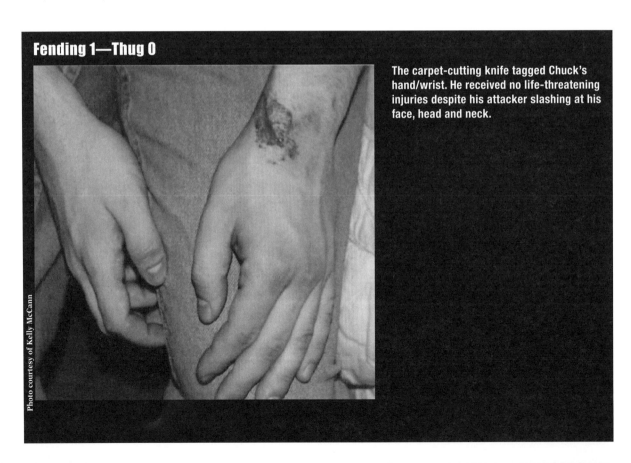

Fending 1—Thug 0

The carpet-cutting knife tagged Chuck's hand/wrist. He received no life-threatening injuries despite his attacker slashing at his face, head and neck.

CHECKING

Fending is defensive in nature, briefly protecting you in order to attack. Checking is offensive in nature; it is a method to physically monitor your attacker while you attack. It's an essential element of continual assessment and one of your training goals. Checking is nothing more than staying attached to your attacker in order to adjust your range, feel what effect your techniques are having on him, render one of his arms or legs useless and monitor what he's doing by feeling his movement. You can apply checking without injury to your attacker or you can slam a check on by striking and then leaving your hand in place.

Sometimes you'll lightly attach yourself to him and other times you'll clamp down hard. It all depends on what kind of attack you launch. For example, I'll lightly attach myself if my plan is primarily striking. I'll clamp down hard when my plan transitions from primarily striking to a takedown or when I need additional leverage.

Checking is an ambiguous skill a bit like Supreme Court Justice Potter Stewart's 1964 cliché about what is and isn't pornographic. He simply said, "I know it when I see it." Apply the concept to checking and don't get wrapped around the axle about particulars—just keep your body in contact with your attacker's once you launch your attack.

I'll go over a couple of specific checks in this section, and the first is the upper-arm check.

To execute: Have your training partner stand in front of you within arm's reach. Index on him to throw an ax hand. When you strike, reach forward with your opposite hand and let it fall to the outside of his arm.

Initially, it's enough to just touch or even be in contact with his arm. Once the fight is on, you can decide whether to clamp down on it or let it go. You'd let a check go if you saw more advantage in striking with your checking hand or if you saw a more advantageous check using another part of your body.

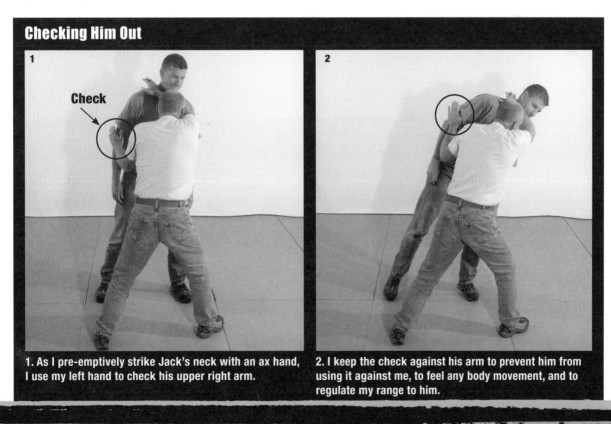

Checking Him Out

1 Check

2

1. As I pre-emptively strike Jack's neck with an ax hand, I use my left hand to check his upper right arm.

2. I keep the check against his arm to prevent him from using it against me, to feel any body movement, and to regulate my range to him.

The next check we'll discuss is the hand hook. You default to the hand hook anytime you're grabbed. You hand hook when your attacker inadvertently gives up one of his hands. Clamp it down to keep it accounted for.

To execute: Have your training partner stand in front of you within arm's reach. Assume an index position. Have him reach across and grab your shirt. As soon as his hand contacts your shirt, drop your same-side hand—the one that's directly across from the arm he reaches with down—onto the junction of his wrist and forearm. For example, if he grabs you with his left hand, drop your right onto his left wrist.

Apply pressure downward with your whole hand. Don't grab his wrist. Keep your thumb extended. You should have him anchored. Simultaneously throw your opposite-side hand forward into his face. In the next chapter, we'll discuss what specifically you can do with the hand you're throwing at his mug. For now, apply your combatives principle No. 13. BaBoom.

The hand hook serves many purposes. It accounts for his hand. It becomes a fulcrum when combined with a violent hip-and-shoulder twist to yank your attacker off-balance. It fouls any attempt to cleanly retract his hand, making it more difficult to reuse against you. If I feel him twist or move away, it transmits his intention. Finally, as I strike him, I'll feel whether my strikes are effective or not if he goes limp or tenses up. The hand hook is a multifunctional check that is truly a default, "go-to" technique anytime someone grabs you.

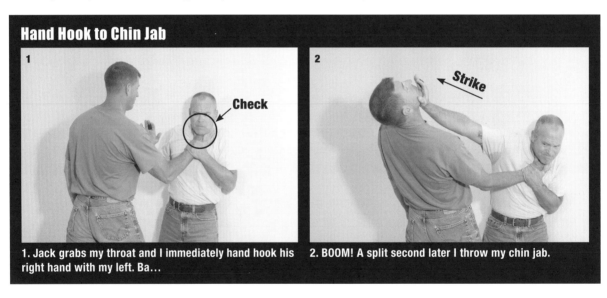

Hand Hook to Chin Jab

1. Jack grabs my throat and I immediately hand hook his right hand with my left. Ba...

2. BOOM! A split second later I throw my chin jab.

There's ample opportunity to check an attacker by the back of his neck as you fight. Some examples are anytime you double him over or when you're cycling elbow strikes or hammerfists to the back of his head. In these situations, your nonstriking hand can be used to monitor what he's doing, and the neck down is the most common. It also flows seamlessly from an ax hand, which you'll learn how to throw in the next chapter. However, for this explanation of necking someone down, refer to the pictures on the following page.

To execute: Have your training partner stand in front of you in a threatening demeanor. Assume an index position that enables you to attack pre-emptively with an ax hand. Have your partner behave aggressively, getting in your face, pointing a finger in it or just getting in your personal space and running his mouth.

When you cook off with your ax hand, after the strike has deposited all its energy, turn your hand to cup the back of your attacker's neck and jerk him downward.

As you continue your attack, reorient your body to his as necessary, but keep your hand on the back of his neck. Reposition your hand as necessary to keep it on the back of his neck. Keep him bent over, off-balance and at a disadvantage.

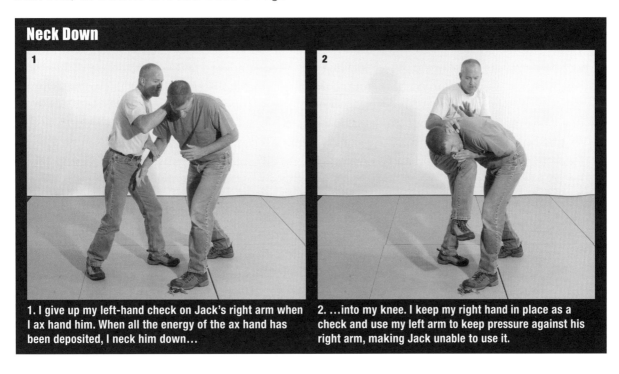

Neck Down

1. I give up my left-hand check on Jack's right arm when I ax hand him. When all the energy of the ax hand has been deposited, I neck him down...

2. ...into my knee. I keep my right hand in place as a check and use my left arm to keep pressure against his right arm, making Jack unable to use it.

There are a lot of ways to check. It's more important that you are checking rather than how you check. For example, if it seems like you're wearing your attacker's T-shirt, I guarantee you're checking him because, whether you know it or not, you're pressing your whole body against him as you take his space. You're also checking when you cycle by reaching forward and slamming your nonstriking hand into your attacker's face and keeping his head turned away between hammerfists. Checking is another skill that demonstrates the simultaneity of combatives.

As I've said, fights are dynamic. Your attacker is fully animated. We can't assume we'll always have the advantage or that we won't be getting beat up ourselves at some point during a fight. That's why we need to maintain a reasonably constant defense while we attack. In order to protect ourselves, we need to discuss how to make an attacker's strikes less effective by blocking.

BLOCKING HAND AND ELBOW STRIKES

I hate to even use the word blocking. In combatives, you block unarmed strikes as a boxer does: through a combination of your guard, your movements, fending and checking. Still, there are times when you've got to block a fist or weapon whistling at your head or stomach because your attacker found or created a momentary opening in your guard. No guarantees right? That also applies to your guard because there's no guarantee you'll be able to avoid or block every one of your attacker's strikes.

Let's talk about how to "block" hand and elbow strikes first. It's preferable to get inside your attacker's strike and just attack. If you can't get inside quickly enough, the second best tactic is to fend the strike—deflecting it *as* you attack. The least preferable but necessary tactic is to absorb the strike somewhere it won't hurt you badly (or a helluva lot less) than if it lands where your attacker's aiming. For example, if you were to throw a punch straight at my face, I'd dip my chin behind my shoulder, twist my waist while leaning sideways to make sure my hand, wrist and forearm are in the way. You may hit my arm or my shoulder but you won't hit my face.

More importantly by getting inside to fend or absorb hand and elbow strikes, you're much less likely to overreact to feints and, consequently, open your guard up unnecessarily. You expect to get hit but you know you're reducing the effectiveness of your attacker's strikes. Protecting yourself this way enables the use of unarmed double taps because blocking is simplified to just an adjustment of your guard. BANG! You go off like a cannon before your attacker's even retracted his hand. *He's* the one open, and *you're* the one capitalizing on it.

To execute: I use "box" drills for teaching a lot of these defensive skills, which is how you'll start learning how to block hand and elbow strikes. So tape out a 3-foot-by-3-foot box on the floor, put on your protective equipment—headgear, mouthpiece, chest protector—and get in the box.

Have your training partner circle you outside the box while throwing strikes at your head and upper body. Stay in your guard and your box. Use all the skills you've learned so far plus movement to deal with his strikes. Look through your guard at your partner. Don't let him bury or beat you down in your guard. If he doubles you over which forces you to take your eyes off of him, it's much more difficult to get back up and into your guard to protect yourself.

Stay in the box but use every inch of it to move forward, backward and from side to side. Hollow out and sway while you adjust your hands and arms as necessary. Fend some strikes and let others impact you somewhere that isn't vital.

After you read the next chapter, incorporate striking back. Have your partner put on his protective equipment and make him pay every time he strikes. Use your guard to cover when he strikes, then explode, answering his one strike with two or three of your own.

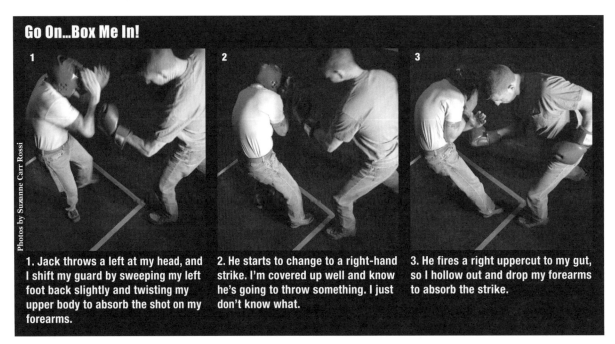

Go On...Box Me In!

1. Jack throws a left at my head, and I shift my guard by sweeping my left foot back slightly and twisting my upper body to absorb the shot on my forearms.

2. He starts to change to a right-hand strike. I'm covered up well and know he's going to throw something. I just don't know what.

3. He fires a right uppercut to my gut, so I hollow out and drop my forearms to absorb the strike.

BLOCKING KNEE STRIKES

Street thugs aren't limited to using only their hands and elbows when they fight; they'll throw knees as well. Because knee strikes use the most powerful muscles in the body—the legs—it's important to know how to block them.

Knee strikes are one of the more versatile infighting strikes. They're hard to see because they're used at very close range and come from below your line of vision. Knee strikes are powerful and can injure you even if you're just trying to block them.

In a standing face-to-face confrontation, you've got to protect your groin from unexpected knee strikes. If you've been beaten down or are doubled over, you've got to protect your thoracic cavity and face from knee strikes. If you take a hard shot and get knocked to your knees, you've got to protect your head and face from your attacker's knees. Let's start by discussing how to block knee strikes to your thoracic cavity and abdomen while still standing.

To execute: Bend over—yeah, I know, bad things always seem to start with that. Your training partner will check the back of your neck and grab the back of your shirt. Have him fire his knee straight up into your chest, which you'll learn is a "knee lift" in the next chapter. Keep your forearms in front of your chest and stomach. Point both your elbows at your waist. Don't hold your forearms against your body. Angle them away slightly to absorb the impact of his knee strikes.

As your training partner increases power and speed, drop one or both of your elbow points into his thigh as it comes up. You'll cause him a lot of pain when you drive your elbows into his thigh muscles. In fact, the harder he throws his knees, the worse it is for him.

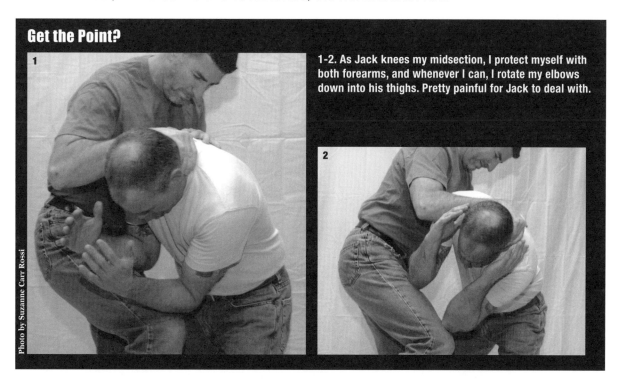

Get the Point?

1-2. As Jack knees my midsection, I protect myself with both forearms, and whenever I can, I rotate my elbows down into his thighs. Pretty painful for Jack to deal with.

Photo by Suzanne Carr Rossi

The next most common knee strike you're likely to encounter and have to protect yourself from is a short-range knee strike to your groin. In contrast to a knee lift, a straight knee is aimed directly at a perpendicular target—your groin. It's an abrupt strike that's difficult to deal with. Since it's one of the most common attacks, it's worth spending some time practicing how to block it.

First, if you're that close to a threat, you should be there on *your* terms. Why are you face-to-face with your hips flat to your attacker's and vulnerable to a groin strike in the first place? Because it's not a perfect world and shit happens. In an ideal situation, you wouldn't let anyone get in your face if they're threatening you. At a minimum, if someone closed on you to get in your face, you'd punch out one hand to stiff arm his chest and use the space you just created to get in guard. But despite your best efforts, you may still find yourself within groin-strike range. You'll only be able to make simple, gross-motor movements to avoid his knee.

To execute: Put on your cup. Stand in the box and assume the hands-up palms-out index. Have your training partner get inside the box with you and get in your face. He should blast his knee straight forward, targeting your groin. Twist your hips to either side.

You'll take the shot on your thigh but will have avoided a direct and powerful strike to your groin. Recognize that your twist chambered you for an immediate retaliatory slashing elbow—perfect for this range. Slashing elbows are covered in the next chapter.

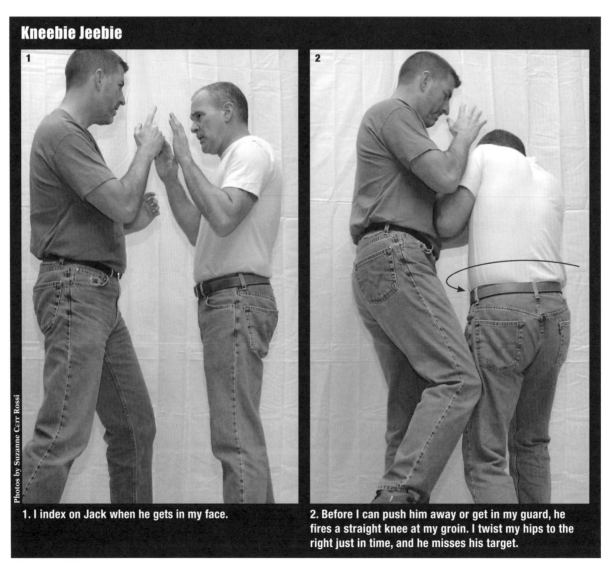

Kneebie Jeebie

Photos by Suzanne Cerr Rossi

1. I index on Jack when he gets in my face.

2. Before I can push him away or get in my guard, he fires a straight knee at my groin. I twist my hips to the right just in time, and he misses his target.

Another natural street fighter's tool you need to be able to defend against is a knee to your head if you've been knocked down. Sometimes, when people get hit hard, they'll stumble and "take a knee" (kneeling down on one knee or genuflecting for you religious types). A half-knocked-out victim, kneeling on the ground, presents a perfect opportunity for a knee to the head.

As I've said, knee strikes are powerful. Catching one in the face or the head can stop the show. Even worse, it's likely an attacker is using a knee to the head when you've already been hurt, so blocking them is a skill worth mastering.

To execute: Back in your box Mister! Take a knee. Have your training partner check the back of your neck and lay his forearm along your back, grabbing your shirt. He should slowly and, with little power, try to strike you in the head with his knee.

Treat his knee to your head as you would any strike. Keep your hands up and articulate your upper body, adjusting your hands and forearms to put as much mass as possible between his knee and your head.

As you grow more confident, put on your headgear and have your partner put his cup on. Start the drill standing in the box with him. Take a knee and have him increase power and speed when he tries to knee your head. Defend but capitalize on the obvious opportunity to strike his groin using unarmed double-tap timing. You'll be at precisely the right height to throw a powerful punch or spearing elbow straight to his family jewels.

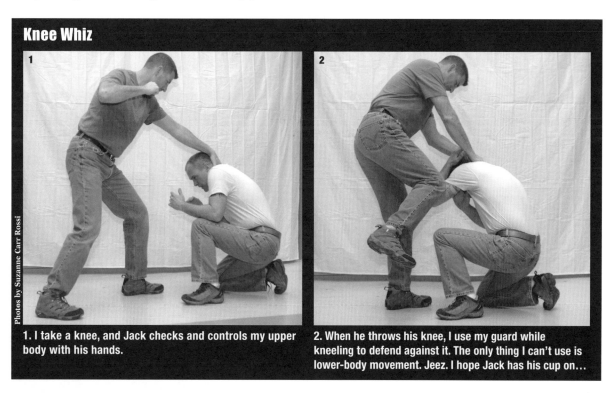

Knee Whiz

1. I take a knee, and Jack checks and controls my upper body with his hands.

2. When he throws his knee, I use my guard while kneeling to defend against it. The only thing I can't use is lower-body movement. Jeez. I hope Jack has his cup on…

BLOCKING KICKS

Although heavily stylized kicks aren't usually found in a street fighter's repertoire, he certainly could and will use his feet. Let's take a look at two of the more likely kicks you'll be confronted with: the front push kick and leg kicks.

Combatives effectively marginalizes a kicker's legs by keeping you inside and too close for an attacker to use kicks. But before you get inside, your attacker may use a push kick aimed at your groin or gut to keep you from closing on him.

Your goal is simply to deflect the push kick and close inside as quickly as possible before the attacker has a chance to recover. No one can kick AND punch at the same time; he'll do neither effectively. For that reason, you want to exploit the opportunity to close while an attacker's still got a foot in the air.

Keep in mind that in combatives, with few exceptions, "blocking" is synonymous with deflecting. You're blocking it off target without the emphasis found in traditional martial arts. Too great a focus on blocking distracts you from attacking. A miss is as good as a mile. If you try to push kick me, I'll give it a little attention by knocking it slightly to the side so I can beat the shit out of you while your foot's still in the air.

To execute: To deflect a push kick, have your training partner stand a couple arm's length away. Assume your guard. Have him step through with his rearmost foot and try to push your groin or abdomen with the ball of his foot.

As he lifts his leg to chamber his push kick, vault in, dropping your opposite-side arm across from the leg he's using. For example, if he's stepping through and kicking you with his right leg, drop your left arm. When you drop your arm, do it forcefully, striking his leg on the inside to deflect it off target. Bend your hand back at the wrist to create a ramp, causing him to swing his leg wide when he drops it.

Simultaneously (there's that simultaneity thing again), twist your hips and shoulder to the right, which improves your range, and drive your other hand into his face. Doing anything with his leg other than deflecting it is secondary to attacking.

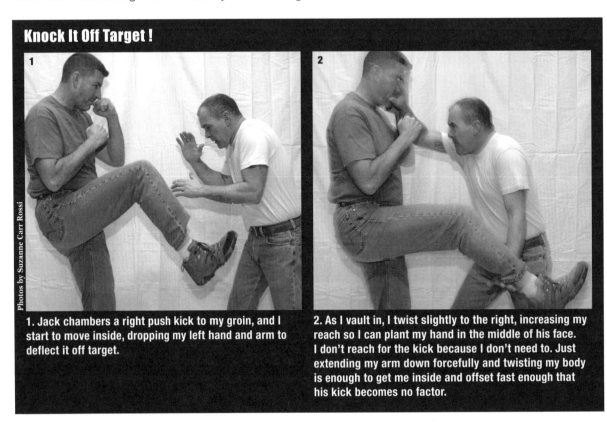

Knock It Off Target !

1. Jack chambers a right push kick to my groin, and I start to move inside, dropping my left hand and arm to deflect it off target.

2. As I vault in, I twist slightly to the right, increasing my reach so I can plant my hand in the middle of his face. I don't reach for the kick because I don't need to. Just extending my arm down forcefully and twisting my body is enough to get me inside and offset fast enough that his kick becomes no factor.

Photos by Suzanne Carr Rossi

Leg kicks have become more popular with the meteoric rise in popularity of MMA. More and more thugs know about them because they see them used in televised competition all the time. They're fairly easy to throw and keep a thug at a comfortable distance from his victim until he can hurt him. A well-thrown leg kick can easily knock an unsuspecting victim down.

If you take two or three hard blasts to your leg from an attacker and don't marginalize them, you're going to start unintentionally reacting even to feints at your legs, which opens you up to head shots.

To execute: You weren't about to step out of that box were you? Get back in there to practice blocking leg kicks! Have your training partner stand outside the box and target your lead leg with a leg kick. I cover how to execute the kick in the next chapter, so have your partner read ahead if he can't figure it out by himself.

As he rolls his hip and unloads his shin into your leg, lift your foot off the ground by raising your thigh and bending your knee. Your leg will have a 90-degree bend in it, and your foot should be a foot off the ground. This technique will absorb the energy of his kick, but the force may spin you slightly. The kick's still going to hurt. However, because you've unweighted your leg and let it swing away, it won't hurt nearly as much *and* your knee can't be injured.

Don't reach down with your hand or arm to block leg kicks. If your hand or forearm gets crushed between his shin and your thigh, something's gonna break, and it won't be his shin. Instead, lift your foot and look for the opportunity to slam your hand into his face that's almost always present when leg kicks are thrown.

Anytime a leg kick lands and hurts you, you can bank on your attacker closing fast to swarm on you. Get your foot back onto the ground quickly after impact and recover your guard.

Charley Horse

Photos by Suzanne Carr Rossi

1. Jack and I set up to practice the defense against leg kicks.

2. When he rolls his hip, I lift my leg, bend my knee and reach my hand forward to hit his face. When I drop my leg, I'm inside his kick and will keep closing.

Even though you're most likely going to see kicks below the waist in street attacks, there's always the chance of someone taking a shot at kicking you in the head if he's able to. Treat high kicks as you would any hand strike to your head. Use your guard and deflect the kick off target or absorb it somewhere you can afford to, like your shoulder.

But don't freak out because whether it's a foot or a hand attack is immaterial. In fact, make your attacker pay dearly for his bad Jackie-Chan impersonation by crashing into him before he's recovered his position. Punish him with the infighting strikes you'll learn in the next chapter.

Now that we've addressed unarmed attacks, let's move on to weapons attacks.

BLOCKING WEAPON ATTACKS

Make no mistake about it, blocking weapons is an advanced skill. There are few universal rules because of the differences in consequence between a stick and an edged weapon. There are considerations unique to each that must be applied depending on what weapon you're attacked with.

Unlike blocking unarmed strikes, weapon blocks are hard blocks. You won't always apply blocks boxing style. Instead, depending on the weapon, you sometimes intercept the arm wielding the weapon to block it's path—hard.

The reason for the different approach is because, once an unarmed strike is deflected or defended against, it ceases to be an immediate risk. Weapons, on the other hand, have a continuing consequence. If you block the actual weapon, as if it were a fist, you're screwed. For example, you throw a punch at me, and I absorb your punch on my forearm and shoulder—no big deal. If you swing a piece of concrete reinforcing bar at me, and I block it with my forearms, you've splintered them—a very big deal.

The same is true in deflecting a fist or a weapon. I pat your punch down, deflecting it from hitting my face, and it hits my shoulder. So what? But, say I deflect your stab to my chest, and it sinks to the hilt in my gut. What the fuck?

BLOCKING STICK ATTACKS

We'll discuss several kinds of weapon blocks in this section, but first let's look at stick attacks.

When I say "stick" I mean anything you swing—a lug-nut wrench, a T-ball bat or a stick or a pipe. It doesn't matter because you're not really going to deal with the weapon; you're going to deal with the arm wielding the weapon.

It's really not a big deal to face someone swinging anything other than an edged weapon at you because they need space to swing it. When you take away the space necessary to swing a weapon, your attacker may as well not have it. You've effectively disarmed him. Whether he swings it as a forehand or backhand swing doesn't matter. CRASH THE GAP and get inside.

Better still, attackers usually get preoccupied trying to use their sticks. They don't branch! That's good news for you because one of your attacker's hands is occupied with something that's harmless to you. You *want* him preoccupied with trying to figure out how to use his T-ball bat when you're married to his chest and kicking the shit out of him. Serves him right.

To execute: Okay. You can come out of your box now. The preferred method of dealing with a stick attack is to immediately render it useless and just vault inside. Now there's no blocking necessary.

Stand in the guard across from your training partner who's armed with a padded training stick. Stay just outside his reach, forcing him to close slightly to hit you with the stick. Have him swing at you as naturally and realistically as possible.

There's obviously some role-playing required because he should behave as an attacker might. He should brandish the stick, wave it around, chamber it and try to strike you. Have him rest it over his shoulder and unexpectedly whip it at you. Mix up how he attacks. He should replicate what he'd do if he were going to attack someone with a stick.

It's your choice when to vault. That means you don't necessarily have to wait for him to attempt to strike you; you could pre-empt. You may decide to wait, but it's up to you based on what scenario he's presenting you with.

When you launch, detonate off your rear foot and stay in your guard. Crash into him using any of the strikes you'll learn in the next chapter. A face mash or spearing elbow works especially well.

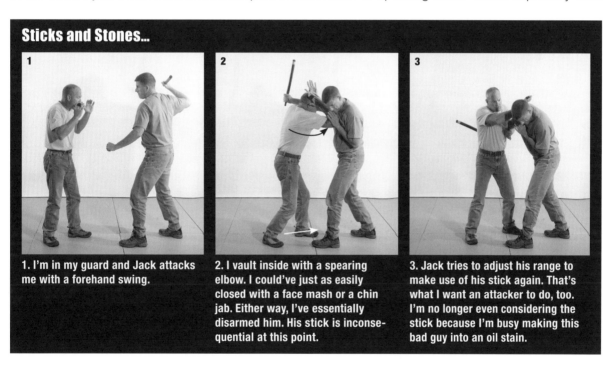

Sticks and Stones...

1. I'm in my guard and Jack attacks me with a forehand swing.

2. I vault inside with a spearing elbow. I could've just as easily closed with a face mash or a chin jab. Either way, I've essentially disarmed him. His stick is inconsequential at this point.

3. Jack tries to adjust his range to make use of his stick again. That's what I want an attacker to do, too. I'm no longer even considering the stick because I'm busy making this bad guy into an oil stain.

When you've got that down (and it shouldn't take long!), try this. Have your partner swing at you with a right-handed forehand swing from a slightly closer distance, as if you were caught off guard. The second you detect threatening movement, vault in and against his swing. For example, if he's swinging at you with his right hand, vault left oblique.

Slam one or both of your forearms into the inside of your training partner's right arm. Keep your blocking forearm(s) perpendicular to his to minimize the chance of it blowing through your block. Look at the pictures on page 118 to see perpendicularity in practice.

You should be able to get inside so quickly that it's impossible for him to develop any real power to swing at all. Keep your forearms slightly angled away—similar to how you held them when you were blocking knees to your chest.

Once you've learned strikes, you'll combine them with blocks using the Styers' beat. BaBOOM! Block and then ax your partner's neck. Block his swing with one arm and use the other to fire a chin jab. You get the picture.

Take His Space

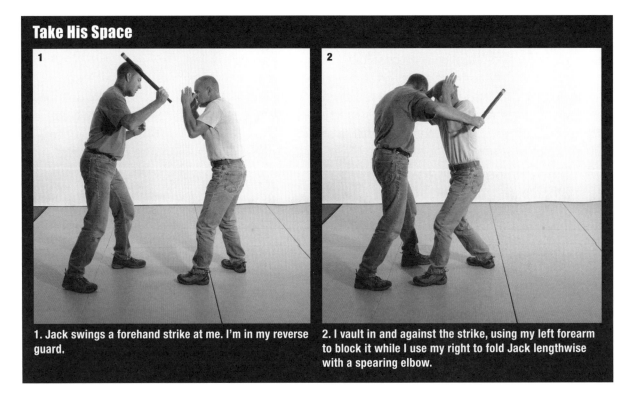

1. Jack swings a forehand strike at me. I'm in my reverse guard.

2. I vault in and against the strike, using my left forearm to block it while I use my right to fold Jack lengthwise with a spearing elbow.

As a final exercise, face away from your training partner at the same distance as before. Have him swing at you twice with a forehand swing followed by an immediate backhand swing. Sway out of the way of the first and vault in before he can get the second off. Stay in your guard with your hands up. Slam your forearms into the back of his arm. Follow up using strikes from the next chapter.

Backhand Blocking

1. I turn around, and Jack swings his stick at my head. I sway back out of the way.

2. I'm recovering my guard as Jack starts to swing back at me.

3. I vault into and against his arm, blocking his strike before he can get it off.

BLOCKING EDGED WEAPONS

There are more issues with countering an edged-weapon attack because dealing with edged weapons while unarmed is sketchy at best. It takes little or no skill to wield a knife effectively—just look at prison techniques. Prison-born edged-weapons techniques are some of the most deadly, yet there's no formal training in them. Conversely it takes an incredible amount of skill to effectively counter a vicious knife attack. It's like a crap shoot.

Here's how I'd prefer to deal with someone wielding a knife:

1. Armed or not, I'd prefer to see the potential problem early and stay well away, avoiding it altogether.

2. If I couldn't avoid the goat-rope altogether, I'd like to be armed and lucky enough to get threatened at an advantageous distance, draw my pistol and verbally warn the thug off. I actually *was* that lucky in Pétionville, Haiti one night years ago. I had the time and space to draw my pistol and warn the thug off. Little prick steadily ran his mouth as he shagged ass.

3. If I couldn't have it happen that way and wasn't armed with a pistol, I'd like to have a less lethal weapon like a collapsible baton or pepper gas *and* the time and opportunity to use them to escape.

4. I don't like the idea of sticking my hand into a Cuisanart, but with no alternative, I'd like to have my folder with me so I could draw it to defend myself. I had to do that in Bogota, Colombia years ago. When my attacker suddenly realized what he'd gotten himself into, he and his cheap-ass-Pakistani-knock-off-Buck-110 ran away.

5. Lastly, if there were no other options, I'd deal with the knifer unarmed. I'd really like that situation to happen in a place with a lot of physical barriers I could put between us. I'd want to frustrate him, running around opposite sides of the obstacles doing the Three Stooges' "Moe, Larry, the cheese!" routine.

Unfortunately, we don't get to pick when, where or how we're attacked and sometimes the guy is on top of you, knife out and in motion before you know anything's going on. I learned that one night outside a hockey game when I was a teenager. Good thing I swayed—my chin was cut so fast with a box cutter that I actually saw the blade in my attacker's hand *after* I was cut and *before* I felt any pain.

You won't get melodrama from me. No gravelly voice saying, "If you're attacked with a knife… expect to get cut…" No shit. No master of the obvious statements like, "Use your pistol if you're attacked with a knife." There's another no-shitter. Everybody understands being attacked with a knife is a pretty dire circumstance.

Truly bad guys? They don't brandish their knives and slash the air. They quickly walk up and stick it in you lots of times. If you back away, they close on you, slashing and thrusting. Don't train for edged-weapon attacks using some ridiculous scenario of a slow, repetitive or stupidly sophomoric pattern that allows you a lot of options. It ain't gonna be that way.

But here's one last thought: If you don't make your attacker tentative about using the knife, you're just prolonging the inevitable. You can't prevail relying on defense alone. You have to alternate between defensive and offensive postures as quickly as the situation allows. Defending against an edged-weapon attack epitomizes the definition of combatives fusion.

Okay, here's a recap of the universals as they apply to edged-weapon attacks:

1. Hurt your attacker before or anytime he tries to hurt you.

2. If you get inside the weapon, trap it, control it, and beat your attacker down.

3. If you can't control it, get outside fast and wait for the next opportunity.

4. If your attacker can't see you, he's less likely to be effective with his knife. Attack his eyes.

5. If your attacker's intent is to kill you and you don't fuck him up quickly and completely, he's going to kill you. Period.

To execute: Both you and your training partner put on your protective equipment—eyewear for you and everything for him. Get back into your box. Have your partner stand outside the box. Start slowly at first.

Have your partner attack with his training blade. He should use a forehand slash on a downward angle across your body. Vault in against the slash and slam both your forearms into the inside of his arm, making sure one impacts his forearm and one impacts above the elbow on his upper arm. Don't cross your arms. Immediately shuffle out. Have him attack on the opposite angle, and you mirror your block, doing it the same way just on the opposite side.

In this exercise, lead with the foot on the same side as the attack. For example, if he slashes at you with his right hand, lead with your left foot. Vault in to get deep. Keep your forearms perpendicular to his.

Cutting Edge

Photos by Suzanne Carr Rossi

1. Jack slashes at me, and I vault in and against his forearm. I'm slamming my ulnas into the inside of his arm. Note how I'm "tabling" my hand by bending it back at the wrist. This prevents Jack's slash from blowing through my block. Knifers don't attack with bullshit slashes. THEY WAIL. If a slash knocks my forearms down, I don't want my forearm, wrist and hand forming a rail to guide it into me. Tabling your hand is like putting a big-ass speed bump in the way—it's a fail safe.

2. Treat a back slash the same way. Keep your forearms perpendicular to your training partner's. Be prepared to withdraw if you can't get control of his arm.

3. Have your training partner stab at your abdomen. Hollow out and drop your forearms down onto his arm as he extends it toward your stomach. Keep your forearms perpendicular to his arm. When he retracts his hand, recover your guard.

I hope you realize none of this shit happens slowly. Your training partner should build speed as you build proficiency. That means "over time." It means that it will take many training sessions and not minutes later in the same training session. You're NOT going to get good at this overnight folks. To handle edged-weapon attacks on the street, you *better* be training hard and at real-world speeds. Have your partner whack the knife fast into your gut, so you learn to snap your arms down lightning fast to hurt his forearm.

Next, have your training partner circle left and right while stabbing and slashing erratically. Build the speed and intensity of his attacks so that they are commensurate with your skill.

Finally, get out of the box and back up against a wall. Put your butt against it, keeping your feet 24 inches or so away. Lean forward slightly. Fuse everything you've learned thus far to both defend and attack as your training partner slashes and stabs at you.

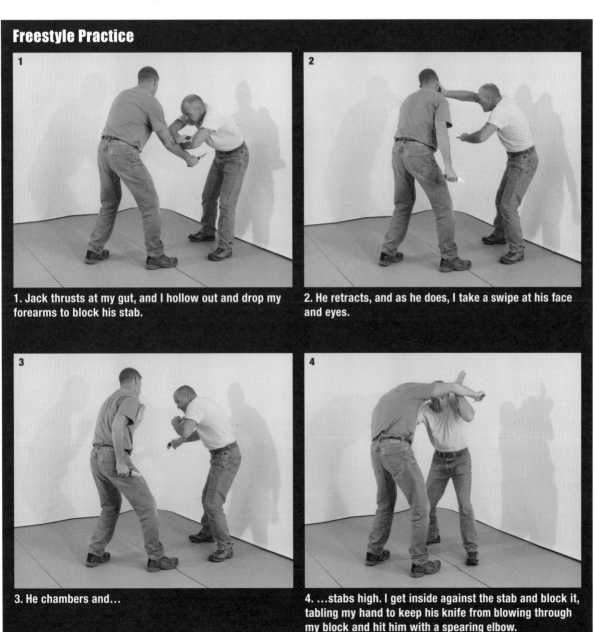

Freestyle Practice

1. Jack thrusts at my gut, and I hollow out and drop my forearms to block his stab.

2. He retracts, and as he does, I take a swipe at his face and eyes.

3. He chambers and...

4. ...stabs high. I get inside against the stab and block it, tabling my hand to keep his knife from blowing through my block and hit him with a spearing elbow.

Here's some ideas to ensure the simultaneity of your defense and offense. Sway back but shin kick or toe kick him when you do. Come off the wall to finger jab him. Hollow out when he slashes at your stomach but throw your hands forward into his face when you do. Spring off the wall to block a slash and ax hand his neck when you withdraw.

Remember, your learning curve intensifies by forcing your use of skills. Limiting your movement by backing against the wall, you're forced to use all your other skills in order to survive.

BLOCK, TRAP AND LOCK

Eventually, your attacker's going to close on you or you'll see an opportunity to close on him and that's when things really get ugly. It's essential to control an edged weapon when you're infighting because they're inherently dangerous when left loose in a close-range attack. Unlike a stick, a knife can be lethal with little to almost no room. Building your skill at trapping and locking is critical to finishing once you're inside.

As you accrue training time, you'll become more efficient at seeing opportunities to exploit. You'll suffer less from the physiological effects of imminent danger because your familiarity with hyperviolence has increased. Let's take a look at how to capitalize on that when we have to deal with blocking a knife attack in order to finish.

To execute: Crash into and against your training partner's right-handed forehand slash. Keep your guard up and slam your forearms into the inside of his arm, **blocking** it. For a second (and I mean a second), he's unable to do anything with it. Without retracting your left arm, just drop it—to the outside of your partner's right—and clamp down onto the back of his upper arm, **trapping** it.

Simultaneously fire your right hand into his neck as you squeeze his right arm against your hip, **locking** it there. Practice following up with either another ax hand or, if you want to adhere to our principles, neck him down into your knee finishing with a hammerfist to the base of his skull.

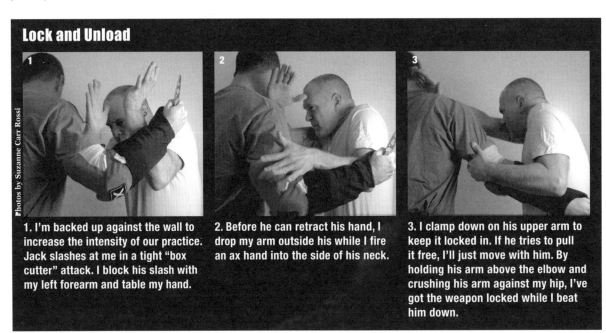

Lock and Unload

1. I'm backed up against the wall to increase the intensity of our practice. Jack slashes at me in a tight "box cutter" attack. I block his slash with my left forearm and table my hand.

2. Before he can retract his hand, I drop my arm outside his while I fire an ax hand into the side of his neck.

3. I clamp down on his upper arm to keep it locked in. If he tries to pull it free, I'll just move with him. By holding his arm above the elbow and crushing his arm against my hip, I've got the weapon locked while I beat him down.

Now have your training partner attack with a right-handed backhand slash. Vault in against it to slam your forearms into the back of his arm, blocking it. Clamp your right hand down on his right wrist, trapping it. Drive your left forearm forward into the back of his arm, locking it.

On the street, you'd also incorporate an out-of-line movement to pull both the attacker's wrist and your hip back as you explode your opposite-side forearm forward and through his arm. You'd apply your full body weight to the effort, blowing out his elbow in the process. You'd also use the environment to slam his head and face down into something completely unpleasant. It's not difficult to hurt someone's elbow when you're using speed, leverage and just being vicious. Amp it up carefully when you practice.

ENVIRONMENTAL ADVANTAGE

Whenever you fight, be aware of all the things around you that can be used to your advantage. You've seen some of these things in the photos already.

Seizing an opportunity to stomp something is another example of environmental advantage. If what you're stomping wasn't on the ground (and it may not be in the very next instant), you couldn't exploit the environmental advantage.

It's a mind-set thing, consider your environment made up of improvised weapons. Instead of swinging these improvised weapons into your attacker, you sling, shove, drive or push *him* into *them*.

Environmental Damage

1. Here's another example. Jack gets me into a front head lock or guillotine choke. I stay situationally aware and am able to drive him forward, slamming his thigh into the point of this table. Works the same way any kick to his leg would, and even better, he doesn't expect it.

2. Jack grabs me in a rear bear hug while I'm standing in a doorway. I slam his arm into the metal edging on the door frame. Remember, all I need is to create some unexpected pain to get some space to exploit to my advantage.

Combatives are about hitting, and hitting means hurting. In fact, combatives are about hitting well to ensure a lot of hurting, so be careful after you uncork the combatives genie. As I said in the beginning of the book, although combatives techniques are not sophisticated, they are the equivalent to a wrecking ball—when swung hard, shit gets broken.

Hitting someone with full-power strikes is going to cause significant trauma; after all, that's the purpose of combatives. But no one actually knows what the result of any particular strike will be simply because there are too many variables that affect the outcome. Use good judgment when you use combatives.

CHAPTER 7
COMBATIVES STRIKES

In a perfect combatives world, each strike is overwhelming and powerful. Unfortunately, that's never the case because fights don't occur in a perfect combatives world. Still, you should make every effort to deliver each strike as effectively as possible.

Effective strikes look and sound like staccato gunshots as they impact. When you watch new students learning to strike, you won't see or hear gunshots. Instead, you'll see "round," dull and noiseless strikes that push against the target instead of hit it. That's because new students haven't refined their technique, so their strikes land with energy leaks. Energy leaks are caused by incorrect body positioning and poor strike structure. Add to that a failure to build gaps, and the result is ineffective strikes that don't maximize the fleeting opportunities I mentioned above. What would be the point of that?

Striking correctly requires you to:

- choose the right personal weapon
- form the weapon correctly
- minimize telegraphic or preparatory movements
- "whip" the weapon into and through the point of impact
- deposit your body weight into the strike
- keep the right structure behind the strike

How important is it to develop good technique? In one study of punching power conducted in England, untrained people punching a 65-pound bag generated only 70 to 100 pounds of force. In contrast, Ricky Hatton, a professional welterweight boxer, generated 900! Spending time learning how to deliver powerful, efficient strikes is well worth your effort because it may be the sole deciding factor when you're fighting for your life.

Based on your personal attributes and as you accrue more training time, you'll start to link strikes together that just seem to flow naturally for you. These are striking "sequences." Effective sequences seem to inherently include many of the combatives principles discussed in Chapter 3. The more inherently applied principles, the better a sequence is likely to be.

Ideally, sequences aren't longer than three strikes. Anything longer would be unrealistic because you'd have to know how your attacker will react to each sequence. Three techniques can be thrown fast enough in succession to hold up no matter what he does. It's the same reason many boxers learn to throw combinations of three punches. You'll notice some sequences in this chapter include takedowns because the strikes naturally set them up. For example:

- right-hand spearing elbow, right-hand face mash, face-mash takedown
- right-hand ax hand, right knee, left-hand slashing elbow
- right-hand shin kick, right-hand slashing elbow, ankle stomp

Don't ingrain your sequences to the point where your reliance on them diminishes your ability to instantly alter course to exploit a sudden, better opportunity. Keep in mind that mastering strikes alone is not enough to make you proficient in combatives. It's achieving the seamless fusion of strikes, movements and positions while applying the combatives principles.

There are continuous yet brief opportunities during any attack when the right strike, thrown the right way and at the right time, *will* overwhelm an attacker. The combatives principles and training goals we've already discussed develop your skill to both create and/or recognize these opportunities. Now let's develop the powerful strikes necessary to capitalize on them.

Combatives strikes are broken down by the personal weapons used to execute them. They include:

- hand strikes
- elbow strikes
- knee strikes
- combatives kicks

FINGER JAB

Finger jabs are hand strikes specifically used to diminish your attacker's sight and to set up additional strikes. If you're an MMA fan, you've no doubt seen the result of an accidental finger in the eye. It's not pretty. The injured fighter immediately stops and jerks backward. His eyelids involuntarily flutter shut while his eyes tear profusely. In combatives, the eyes are a *persistent primary target*.

A finger jab is usually thrown with the closest hand to the attacker's face and is an abrupt, explosively fast strike shot directly into his eyes. It's delivered as fast as possible and is one of the few times you sacrifice some power for speed. Finger jabs can stop even the most committed attacker in his tracks, making them a no-brainer. Get to your attacker's eyes early, quickly and repeatedly.

To execute: Abruptly snap your arm straight out as you would a jab in boxing. Keep your hand open with your fingers slightly curved and splayed. Keeping your fingers splayed improves your chances of hitting both of the attacker's eyes instead of just one. Your hand should be slightly angled, like a plane on its final approach for landing. This prevents your fingers from hyperextending on impact.

Finger Jab Practice

1. Jack's holding a muay Thai forearm shield up and about an arm-and-a-half's length from my face so I can practice my finger jab. From the guard, I snap my hand forward into the pad.

2. In actual use on the street, it's not uncommon for your palm to smash an attacker's nose, crushing it.

The Finger Jab in a Scramble

You can use finger jabs pre-emptively during an attack no matter if you're standing or on the ground. Continuously attack the eyes to disrupt your attacker's vision by making his eyes tear profusely and involuntarily slam shut.

HAMMERFIST

Hammerfists are a great default hand strike for hitting anything in the way, like a face, head, neck, arm or back. They feel very natural to use and protect your hand because they're delivered with the side of your fist, which is the meatiest part.

Hammerfists are big, gross-motor movements that are more than just powerful; they cycle well, also. From a hands-up palms-out index position and without telegraphing your intent, simply smash your hammerfist down into your attacker's face as you vault in.

To execute: To hide tremor and prevent any preparatory movements that telegraph your intent, move your hands vaguely, like you're trying to calm your attacker down as he runs his yap. Explode off whichever foot is most natural for you given the hand you're using to strike. Keep your hand open, flat to the surface of your attacker's face, and your arm relaxed until *just* before impact. At the last second, snap your hand sideways (thumb toward your face) and close your fist. Don't form your fist too early, that'll only slow your hand speed down and result in a less powerful strike.

Keep your forearm perpendicular to the ground and centered on your attacker. Don't let your elbow angle outward or you'll lose power.

Maximize your power by crouching slightly as you vault in. Drop your weight into the strike as your lead foot lands.

Don't lead with your head, stay upright and check your attacker with your opposite hand as you close.

When you cycle hammerfists, fully articulate your arm through the arc of the strike, then pull the hammerfist through to chamber for each repetition. Whip your fist around to gather momentum and then slam it back into your attacker. Don't mimic hammering a nail. Your chambering movement is much bigger, more like winding up and throwing a baseball.

Hammerfist Practice

Strike through the pad. Visualize your hand hitting your knee.

The Hammerfist from Hell

1. Chamber your hammerfist as big as the space available and the circumstance allows. This shot is chambered to hit Jack's floating ribs if he gets rambunctious.

2. I've got Jack doubled over and check him with my left hand on the back of his neck. I just keep replacing my check with my hammerfist to cycle. Remember our combatives principles in Chapter 3? Repetitive strikes are like pistons on a camshaft, if Jack gets froggy I'll retract my check and drop the hammerfist.

FACE MASH

A face mash—yep another hand strike—is executed the same as a hammerfist except your hand stays open, allowing a larger area of it to contact on impact. Face mashes slam into your attacker's face and forcefully snap his head back while smashing his nose and his eyes. It's a more comprehensive head strike than a finger jab or the hammerfist, which are used to concentrate striking force in only one area.

A face mash explodes into your attacker's face and transfers a tremendous amount of force directly into his face and head. Don't bother trying to cycle face mashes because they just don't work well ergonomically.

The best follow-up technique for a face mash is a takedown. Just transition your ever present upper-arm check to a trap and don't retract your other hand from the attacker's face after the strike. Instead, pull his arm toward you and lift the elbow of the arm you mashed him with. Shove his face back, rotating his head backward and down. Shuffle forward quickly to maintain contact as he falls. You can follow up the takedown with an armbar. Or you can just let go, and he'll fall onto the ground.

To execute: Read the instructions above on how to hammerfist. Don't close or turn your hand. Done.

Face-Mash Practice

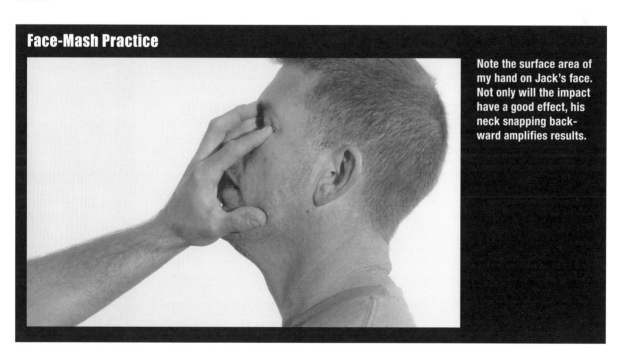

Note the surface area of my hand on Jack's face. Not only will the impact have a good effect, his neck snapping backward amplifies results.

Face Mash Madness

1. I end this stick disarm with a violent vertical face mash, slamming Jack's head sideways into the deck.

2. You can see the effect using face mashes has on Jack in this photo. He's turned his head away, making it difficult to reorient on me, while I chamber another right-hand elbow strike.

REACTION SPEED AND REGULATING FORCE

In addition, because the movement you make for the face mash is similar to the strike movement of the jugular/clavicle-notch attack, finger jab, hammerfist and chin jab, your reaction speed and time greatly improve.

For example, if someone grabs your shirt, all you have to do is clamp a hand hook on and throw your opposite hand forward. The level of threat determines what strike you'll form your hand for and its trajectory. From this position, you can do one of the following—from least injurious to most injurious—to an attacker:

1. Attack the attacker's jugular or clavicular notch and take him to the ground.
2. Finger jab his eyes and make him jerk away from you with disrupted vision.
3. Face mash him or slam his head into the ground with the face-mash takedown.
4. Hammerfist his face.
5. Chin jab him.

AX HAND

An ax hand is a penetrating hand strike best used on the sides of an attacker's neck, face, front of his throat or base of his skull. It's also a useful technique to disengage from grabs and use during other situational self-offense sequences on an attacker's forearms.

To execute: Vault off the foot opposite to your striking hand at an oblique angle. Vault into your attacker and in the direction of your strike. Your weight drops as your lead foot falls. On impact, shrug your hips and shoulder violently to unload as much torque as possible into the strike. Visualize your ax hand cutting through your attacker.

Keep your arm and hand relaxed as they whip toward your attacker. On impact, thrust your thumb outward, stiffening your entire hand like you're saluting but with your thumb extended. This prevents the weapon (your hand) from collapsing in the middle on impact and subsequently not being stiff enough to penetrate deeply into the target.

Aim your strike deep. If you try to put your hand *exactly* on the side of your attacker's neck, you could miss altogether if he pulls back slightly. The margin for error is too small. On the other hand, if you aim deep, you're strikes are more likely to land perfectly. If the attacker doesn't pull back, you're going to clock him with some point along your forearm. All good.

Ax-Hand Practice

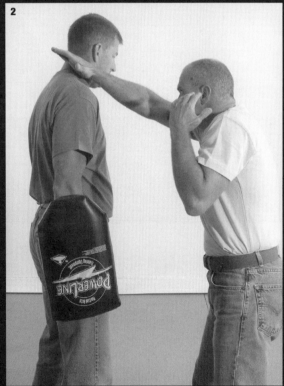

1. I push off my left foot in the direction of the strike, keep my left guard hand up and whip the strike into the pad. Note that I'm pushing my weight into the strike. Also, look at my right foot. It's going to land just as my strike impacts.

2. This hand placement is optimal, but if I hit Jack with my forearm, that's okay too. The point is to get the strike off in time and with power. If it's not perfect, don't sweat it. Fire off some more!

In a perfect world, you'd want to concentrate maximum power into the smallest impact area of any target to penetrate as deeply as possible. But you're not fighting in a perfect combatives world; you're fighting a crackhead with a knife on the corner of Shithouse Road and 32nd Ave. It's better to hit an attacker and achieve an 80-percent effect than to miss him because you tried for perfect hand placement and got a zero-percent effect instead. Don't wait for the perfect opportunity to fire the perfect shot because it may never appear.

Ax-Hand Attack

Here's another use of the ax hand. I complete this disarm by ripping the pistol from Jack's grip as I slam his soft tissue with my ulna by using an ax-hand movement.

CUPPED-HAND STRIKES

The cupped-hand strike specifically targets the ears of your attacker. It works well because the result is terrible, intense pain when you rupture your attacker's eardrum or cause "acoustic trauma." The cupped hand is a powerful, fast technique similar to a correctly-thrown hook in boxing.

To execute: Put your fingers and thumb together. Bend your knuckles slightly and cup your hand as you would to scoop water out of a bucket. Keep your hand relaxed, and tense your shoulder on impact while "shrugging" the strike through the target. Don't lift your elbow as you strike.

You vault off the same-side foot in the direction of the strike and on an oblique angle into your attacker. Violently twist your hips and upper body on impact.

Cupped-Hand Practice

1. Displacing air quickly around the ear increases the effectiveness of cupped-hand strikes and is accomplished by creating a pocket of air between your hand and the surface you're striking. Keep your thumb and fingers together and arch your palm slightly.

2. As I hit the pad, I keep my elbow down to create the proper structure behind the strike. I use hip and shoulder snap to increase my power. Because you strike through your target, you're automatically chambered for an immediate ax hand in the opposite direction when the strike's complete.

If you miss your attacker's ear and hit the side of his neck instead, you're still going to rock him. If you hit the side of his head, you'll snap his head sideways and that puts the hurt on him as well.

Cupped-Hand Chaos

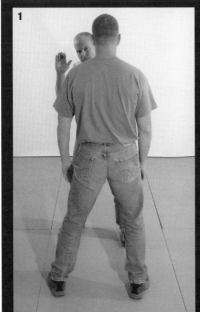

1. I index on Jack.

2. I take a short explosive step in the direction of the strike and plant one on the side of Jack's head and neck, twisting my hips into it and slightly pivoting as I follow through.

3. Sweeet! Check out Jack "Crazy Legs" Stradley!

CHIN JAB: A COMBATIVES CLASSIC

The chin jab is a classic combatives hand strike. It's a dangerous strike used in dire circumstances. A chin jab explosively snaps your attacker's head back on his neck like it's on a swivel. The potential for a serious neck injury is significant. If the attacker's head is slightly turned and his mouth is open when you hit him, the chin jab may break his jaw. It's likely to shatter some teeth making him spit Chiclets, and if his tongue *was* in the way, it won't be after the chin-jab. It'll be on the ground.

The chin jab is an excellent technique to deal with two-handed finger chokes, lapel grabs and other close, imminently dangerous situations when you believe you are in immediate jeopardy.

To execute: From the guard position, crouch slightly and vault straight in at your attacker. Bend your hand back at the wrist as if you were resting a barbell in your palm and getting ready to bench-press 200 pounds. Explosively jam your palm up and under your attacker's chin, using the same level of effort you would to bench-press your max weight, and fully extend your arm. Abruptly straighten your legs slightly as you strike to maximize your power. Stay upright.

Chin Jab Chiclets

1. You can see how to form your hand clearly in this photo.

2. Don't restrict your range of movement when you fire a chin jab. If the situation is dire enough to use a chin jab, let it rip! Extending your arm explosively and completely will overwhelm any resistance of the neck, resulting in significant injury.

Here's a good mental image: Imagine someone much taller than you pressing you up against a wall with both their hands wrapped around your throat. Now visualize clamping a hand hook on one of his arms. Fire your chin jab with the other hand right up his centerline and underneath his chin. As his head snaps back, fully extend your arm and twist your shoulder forward to get even more depth.

Yup. Spittin' Chiclets.

Chin-Jab Knee Sequence

1. Jack snaps violently back, shooting his hips forward…

2. …making my straight knee even more effective as I crash it into his groin.

Note: Work on your timing when you practice this sequence. Retract your chin jab as you fire your knee up in the Styers' beat rhythm—BaBoom. Also be careful because the groin shot will cause the attacker's head to shoot straight at you.

SPEARING ELBOW

Elbow strikes are a fantastic infighting weapon because they're powerful and need little room to chamber. The spearing elbow is one of the most powerful and painful strikes in combatives. It emanates naturally from the guard, making it an extremely useful and fast technique to crash into your attacker with.

The spearing elbow is even more powerful and painful when an attacker closes hard and fast on you. Faced with a haymaker, a forehand stick attack or a front bear hug, exploit the opportunity with a spearing elbow. You'll fold your attacker in half—lengthwise.

To execute: Suddenly and explosively, vault directly at your attacker, whipping your weapon-side hand along the contour of your head to index your elbow straight ahead. Drive your elbow point straight into your attacker's chest. The spearing elbow is a true, full body-weight strike that concentrates all your power into a very small area.

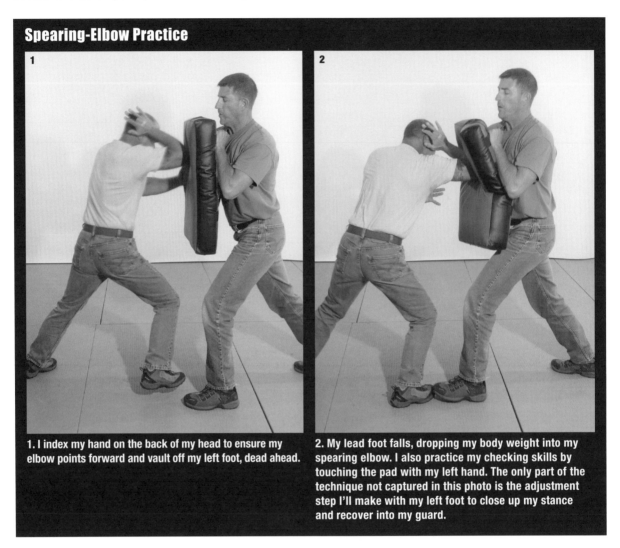

Spearing-Elbow Practice

1. I index my hand on the back of my head to ensure my elbow points forward and vault off my left foot, dead ahead.

2. My lead foot falls, dropping my body weight into my spearing elbow. I also practice my checking skills by touching the pad with my left hand. The only part of the technique not captured in this photo is the adjustment step I'll make with my left foot to close up my stance and recover into my guard.

Don't reach toward your attacker with your elbow or bend at your waist. Stay upright and crash into him with your whole body, leading with your elbow tip.

I usually default to my strong-side elbow so I can instantly transition to an ax hand to hack my attacker's neck. My opposite hand always defaults from my guard to a check and then transitions to a trap or lock. Like any combatives technique, I visualize driving the point of my elbow straight out the back of whatever I'm striking.

The adaptability of this strike from the guard, its inherent power and the pain it creates make it a no-brainer.

Spearing Elbow vs. Punching Attack

1-3. In this sequence, Jack closes on me intending to throw a punch. I vault in with a spearing elbow, folding him up, then transition to an ax hand.

SLASHING ELBOW

The slashing elbow is a fast, violent, short-range strike used to attack the brachial-plexus region (the junction of the neck and shoulder), face, head and base of the skull. Its utility is most apparent in tight quarters, during clinches and on the ground. Few people expect you to strike with an elbow making it even more useful.

Slashing elbows are extremely powerful because they involve full body movement. They also cycle well ergonomically.

To execute: From the guard, vault forward off the same-side foot as your slashing elbow and on an oblique angle in the direction of the strike. Use your off hand to snatch the attacker's upper arm in order to check him during the strike. Let the slashing elbow rip through its complete range of movement in an arc, ending on what you want to hit.

Fully articulate your shoulder in order to point your elbow tip at the sky. This ensures you strike diagonally downward and into your attacker as opposed to horizontally swiping at him. Keep your hand loose and index your extended thumb on your sternum to keep your rotation correct.

Your weight should drop when your elbow tip impacts on the attacker. Follow through with the strike, driving your elbow down and into your attacker. Shuffle forward to stay within range of him because he's almost certainly going to stumble backward.

Slashing-Elbow Practice

1. Seeing a slashing elbow from the rear provides a more complete understanding of how to get it right. I'm in a reverse guard. Notice my strong-side hip is slightly to the rear.

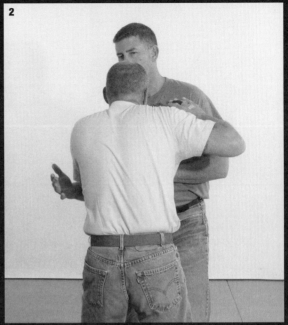

2. As I initiate this pre-emptive slashing elbow, I check Jack's right upper arm into my left hand and begin to rotate my elbow up.

3. I point my elbow tip up in order to create the correct angle to slash down with. I monitor Jack's movements with my check to keep me within striking distance. My right hip isn't rearward anymore because I'm twisting my hip and shoulder to maximize my power.

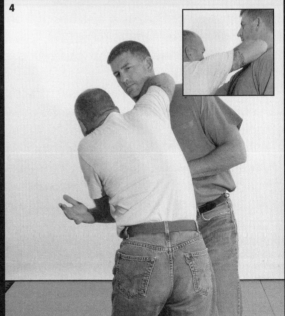

4. I slash downward at a rough 45-degree angle. I'd prefer to hit the junction of his neck and shoulder, but this strike is going to hurt anywhere it lands.

Styers' Beat + Slashing Elbow = Survival

1. This situation needs quick thinking and quick action. It's perfect for the Styers' beat and a slashing elbow. I've got to quickly prevent Jack from successfully drawing his pistol and disable him. BaBoom.

2. I twist my shoulders left and slam my hand down on top of his, fouling his attempt to draw his gat. Ba...

3. BOOM! Keeping my left hand on top of his, I pivot on my left foot and sling a full-body-weight slashing elbow onto the junction of Jack's neck and shoulders. As fast as you can say, " BaBoom," I'm on my way to controlling this dangerously close confrontation.

If you merely swipe at your attacker with your elbow (moving it horizontally), even a minor movement away will result in "a swing and a miss." Make sure you get your elbow tip up and strike diagonally down and into an attacker when you close.

STRAIGHT KNEE

Now let's talk about using our knees. A straight knee drives forward into targets that are perpendicular to the ground. Targets for a straight knee include the common peroneal nerve, the groin, the femoral nerve or your attacker's face, if he's kneeling or sitting on the ground.

To execute: Vault off the foot you won't strike with into your attacker, leading with your striking knee and not your head. Cantilever slightly, staying in your guard and driving your knee forward. Don't lift your knee into your attacker because you're generating power from your vault and your body weight. Instead, if you attack with your body, your knee just happens to be what's impacting with your attacker. Just like the spearing elbow, your knee points straight ahead.

Straight knees are powerful and fast strikes that are easy to execute by using your full body weight. Be prepared to slam a face mash into it or ax hand his neck. Keep your face off axis from his to protect against a collision.

Straight-Knee Practice

1. From the reverse guard, I have a naturally occurring gap between my strong-side knee and my training partner's groin. Note that Jack's head is turned and slightly to the side to protect himself in training.

2. I explode off my nonstriking foot and exploit the gap, utilizing my full body-weight to slam my knee straight into what would be Jack's groin. My guard is tight, and I use my left hand to hack the side of Jack's neck with an ax hand. I'm upright and am careful not to lead with my head.

Straight Knee...SCORE! (SUV Gets the Assist)

1. Using an environmental advantage, I trap Jack's head against the bumper of this vehicle so his head will absorb the full impact of my chambered straight knee.

2. Sucks to be Jack.

KNEE LIFT

Knee lifts strike targets that are parallel to the ground. You'll use them in situations like when your attacker's doubled over or when his groin is directly beneath your knee.

A knee lift drives your knee upward instead of forward. Because of that, you always want to chamber as much as possible. You need to create a bigger gap to achieve greater momentum. It's much harder to use body-weight striking with a knee lift because you can't efficiently project your body weight upward.

At the same time, you also need to control your attacker to prevent him from posturing up, which could result in a glancing impact. Keep his thoracic cavity parallel to the ground to create a perpendicular surface for your knee lift to impact on. Still, when you chamber big, knee lifts hurt an attacker even if he manages to block them with his forearms.

To execute: Maintain control of your attacker and push the two of you apart to create a gap; fully extend your leg to chamber. Using as much violence of action as possible, crash the gap and jerk him into your knee lift as you drive it forward and upward into him.

Knee-Lift Practice

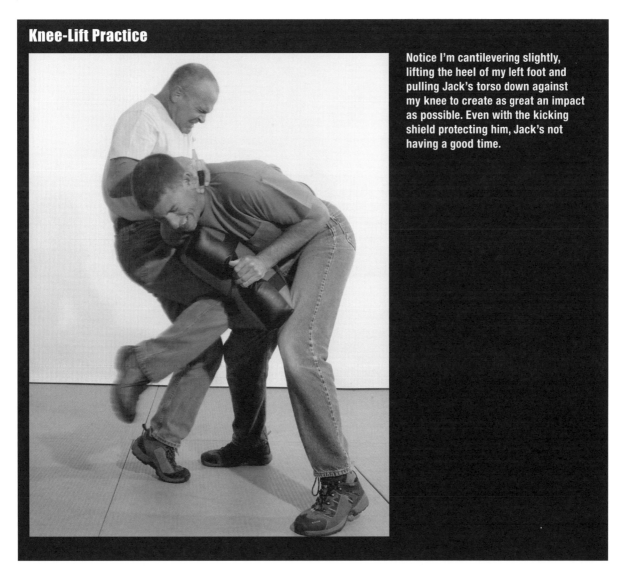

Notice I'm cantilevering slightly, lifting the heel of my left foot and pulling Jack's torso down against my knee to create as great an impact as possible. Even with the kicking shield protecting him, Jack's not having a good time.

If your knee strike has good effect on the target, cycle it. If not, drop your foot between your attacker's legs to take his space and follow up with a slashing elbow or hammerfist. Hey! You just applied another combatives principle by alternating low line and high line attacks. You also branched from your knee attack to another!

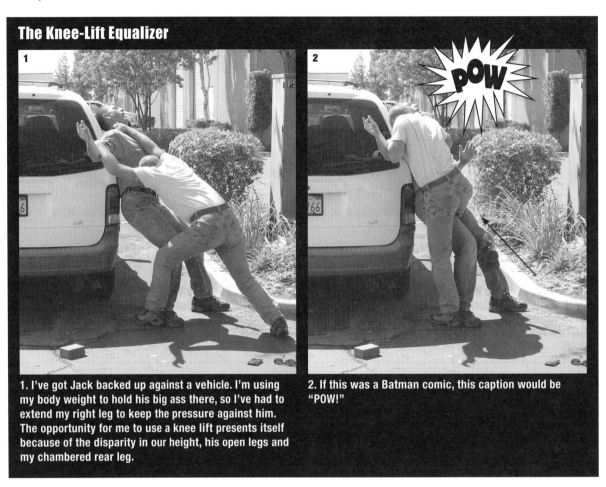

The Knee-Lift Equalizer

1. I've got Jack backed up against a vehicle. I'm using my body weight to hold his big ass there, so I've had to extend my right leg to keep the pressure against him. The opportunity for me to use a knee lift presents itself because of the disparity in our height, his open legs and my chambered rear leg.

2. If this was a Batman comic, this caption would be "POW!"

SHIN KICK

Combatives kicks target below the waistline because they can be executed without too much worry of getting out of position or off-balance.

As my old man would say, "This is a corker of a kick!" It's a little challenging to describe well though. A shin kick isn't a shin rake. Shin rakes occur when you rake the edge of the sole of your boot down someone's shin. They aren't nearly painful enough to be meaningful and end up momentarily putting your feet too close together, subjecting you to being tripped or pushed off-balance.

A shin kick, on the other hand, is a nasty strike. It's an angular stomp, down and through your attacker's shin and delivered with the inside of your boot.

To execute: Use the foot directly across from the attacker's shin you want to kick. Lift your leg up by bending your knee. Point your toe outward. Step across and toward your attacker. Jam the inside edge of your boot into your attacker's shin at roughly a 45 degree angle.

As you jam your foot down, extend your leg into his shin. Crouch slightly as if you were doing a stomach crunch, bending the opposite knee to help drop your weight into his shin. Visualize it going through his shin and splintering it.

You'll normally get one of two results from a shin kick: Your attacker's leg hyperextends at the knee, making him fall backward and onto the ground. Or his leg will get blown out from under him, and he'll fall forward.

You're using both your crouch *and* the extension of your kicking leg to deposit all your power through your attacker's shin. It's not uncommon for a guy to vomit from this kick because of the sharp and terrible pain.

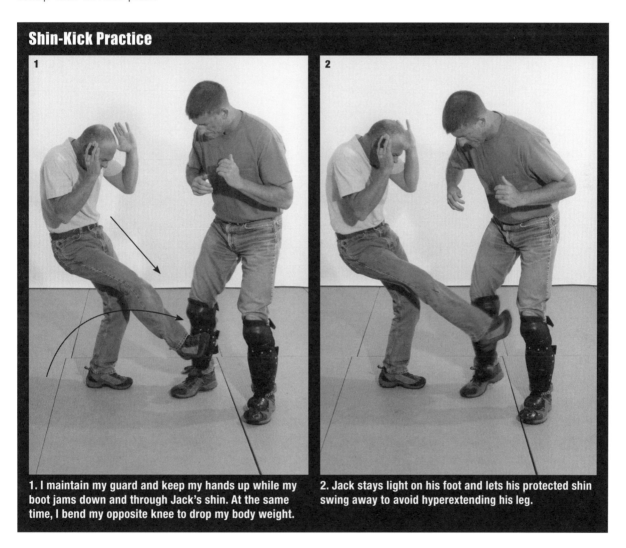

Shin-Kick Practice

1. I maintain my guard and keep my hands up while my boot jams down and through Jack's shin. At the same time, I bend my opposite knee to drop my body weight.

2. Jack stays light on his foot and lets his protected shin swing away to avoid hyperextending his leg.

Don't kick *at* the shin by using a sideways swipe of your leg like you're dribbling a soccer ball. Stomp down through it on an angle.

Off-the-Wall Shin Kick

Jack's backed me up against a wall, and I have to use all my combatives movements and combinations to protect myself. I make him pay for trying to grab me by shin kicking his leg and hyperextending it.

TOE KICK

The toe kick is a fast, sharp kick to your attacker's groin with the upturned toe of your boot. It's an effective kick partially because it originates from below the attacker's line of vision and partially because most people don't expect kicking attacks from very close range. The beauty of a toe kick is that if you miss with the toe of your boot, you'll hit the attacker no matter what with your instep, shin or knee, depending on the range.

The toe kick is a great technique to use when you sway back to clear your attacker's fully-committed strike, slash or swing. He's also unwittingly creating a really bad head-on car crash—his groin and your foot! When the toe kick lands, it has a great effect because it's a penetrating and deep kick to his nut sac.

To execute: Standing in the forward guard, violently lift your rear foot forward and up by raising your thigh toward your chest. Keep your leg bent at a 90-degree angle and lift the toe of your boot. Cantilever backward just slightly to drive the toe of your boot deeper into your attacker's sac.

Because this is a close-range kick, don't lead with your head. Also, make sure you offset your head to one side or another of your attacker's head. Return your foot to where it was or, to start pressuring him, drop it between his legs and strike him with a slashing elbow or hammerfist.

Toe-Kick Practice

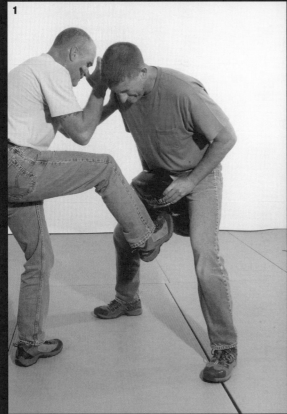

1. From a forward guard, I create a little gap to lift my toe kick through. My toe is upturned and I'm keeping my right hand up in the guard. My left hand is already checking Jack's shoulder. Note that my leg is kept bent on impact.

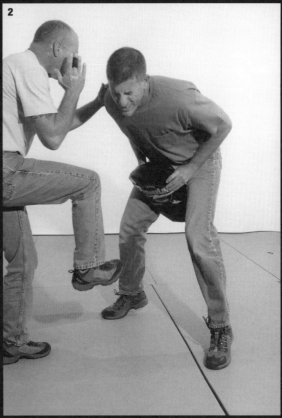

2. This photo is actually my foot being dropped immediately after the kick. I used it here because you haven't seen nearly enough pictures of Jack in terrible pain.

ANGLE/HOOK KICK

Don't confuse this kick with a muay Thai leg kick or a Pressure Point Control Tactics (PPCT) law-enforcement angle kick. The angle/hook kick is specifically designed to damage the knee and break the attacker's base, driving him to the ground. It also penetrates deep into the common peroneal nerve, which creates significant pain.

To execute: Lift up the foot opposite the one you intend to kick by bending your knee. Point your heel upward. Pivot and roll your hip over as you slash your shin down at a 45-degree angle through the outside of your attacker's knee.

Angle/Hook-Kick Practice

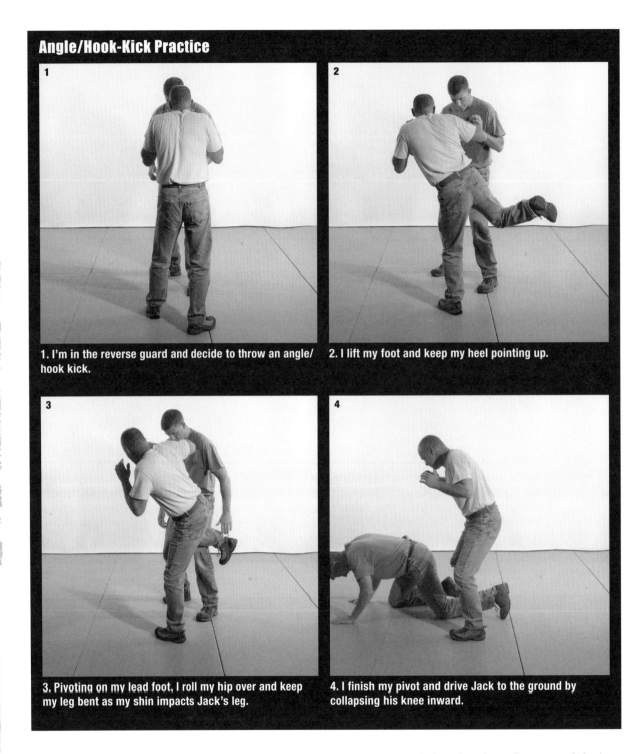

1. I'm in the reverse guard and decide to throw an angle/hook kick.

2. I lift my foot and keep my heel pointing up.

3. Pivoting on my lead foot, I roll my hip over and keep my leg bent as my shin impacts Jack's leg.

4. I finish my pivot and drive Jack to the ground by collapsing his knee inward.

On impact, DRIVE your shin down and through your attacker's leg, leaning all your weight into it. Stick your leg to his and force him down to the ground while staying upright. This structural kick breaks your attacker's base by collapsing his knee inward. The angle/hook kick is a bent leg kick. Don't straighten your leg when you execute it.

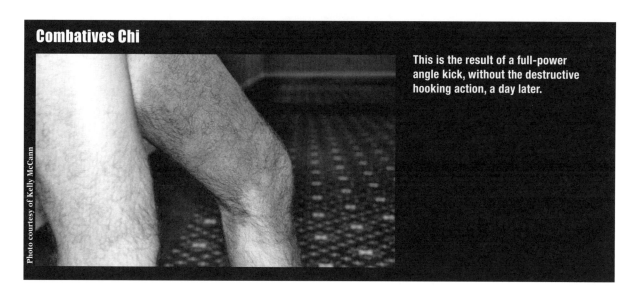

Combatives Chi

This is the result of a full-power angle kick, without the destructive hooking action, a day later.

THE STOMP

In combatives, we stomp on hands, elbows, upturned ankles, flat ankles, knees, and in the worst of situations, heads. Stomping generates huge amounts of force and is incredibly effective because what you're stomping is on an immovable surface—the ground—with no give. Stomping is a completely destructive and damaging technique.

Stomping Practice

1. An upturned heel always indicates a great opportunity to stomp. To chamber my stomp, I bring my thigh toward my chest and bend my leg.

2. When I stomp down onto the target, I also crouch slightly to drop my weight into it. Don't fully extend your leg or you may, in your fury, hyperextend it on impact.

Note: Don't stomp on things you don't mean to break.

To execute: This won't be hard to explain. Have you ever stood a can on end and stomped it flat? There you go. Imagery is everything!

Standing over what you intend to stomp, lift your leg bending your knee. As you lift your leg, straighten the opposite leg. When you stomp onto your target, crouch slightly in order to drop all your weight into it and extend your stomping leg partially. Leaving your leg slightly bent avoids hyperextending it on impact.

If your attacker's down, and lacks the good sense to quit while he's ahead, visualize a can on his ankle, knee, elbow or wrist and stomp it. He'll get the whole "quitting thing" pretty quickly.

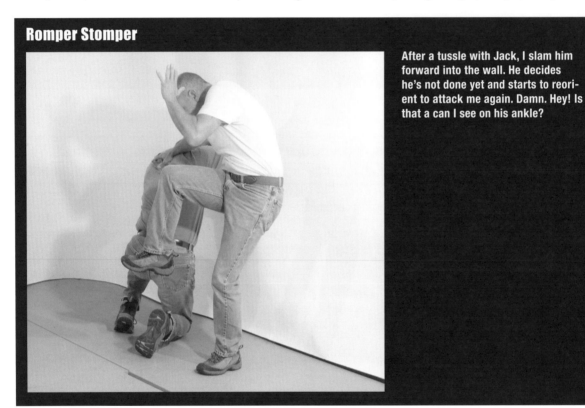

Romper Stomper

After a tussle with Jack, I slam him forward into the wall. He decides he's not done yet and starts to reorient to attack me again. Damn. Hey! Is that a can I see on his ankle?

LOW DESTRUCTIVE KICK

The low destructive kick is an excellent tool to permanently break your attacker's base and make him nonambulatory. Use it anytime during a struggle in which you find yourself in front of and slightly offset from your attacker, facing opposite directions. You can create the opportunity to kick from any number of situations. For example, you've just fired a couple vicious knee lifts into your attacker and simply swing your leg outside instead of inside to use a low destructive kick to destroy his knee.

To execute: During a fight there will be several opportunities to use the low destructive kick. It's not an opening technique because the movement to initiate it is too telegraphic. It's a great infighting technique.

Maintaining contact with your attacker's upper body, lift your leg that's opposite the leg you intend to kick and swing it up to chamber. When you start to extend your foot toward his knee, twist your hip and shoulder to increase your power delivery.

Low-Destructive Kick Practice

1. I rock Jack with an ax hand during a sequence. He stumbles, falling away from me. Instead of sticking to him as I normally would, I see the opportunity to break his base with a low destructive kick.

2. Staying connected to him with my hands, I chamber my leg.

3. I kick downward and inward at a 45-degree angle into the outside of his knee.

4. I drop my weight into it and extend my leg, breaking Jack's base and collapsing his knee. Damn! Is that another can I see on his ankle?

Crouch into the kick and extend your leg, using a snapping action. Be careful to not let your foot be trapped by his leg when his knee collapses as he falls down. *Do* drive your foot into his leg forcing him down to the ground.

Inside Low-Destructive Kick

1. Jack's up close and personal and starts to draw his pistol on me.

2. I snap my foot down against his knee and foul his draw. He starts to fall away and tries to regain his balance.

3. My kicking action has too great an effect on his knee and ankle, which causes him to go down hard.

SUMMARY: DEFENSIVE ~~KILLS~~ OOPS, I MEAN SKILLS

Sometimes it's incredibly difficult to get concepts and techniques across in a book. It's frustrating for me to write all this without being able to get out on a mat with you and literally bang it out. But trust me. With a little training and practice, these things will become apparent quickly. They'll happen so easily and naturally that it'll be hard for you to believe. Remember, time spent going slow at first comes back threefold in speed later. Be patient.

You'll increasingly understand that the key to making combatives work is a ruthless combatives mind-set. Especially with edged weapons, you've got to make your attacker pay a price for trying to stick you. If you don't, you'll end up defending yourself to death, literally.

Don't get frustrated or grow disheartened. Whenever you start training really intensely, things seem to happen too fast to get a handle on. You'll ask yourself, "How the HELL am I supposed to get all that done in the blink of an eye?" The answer is that it's actually longer than the blink of an eye.

It's like when you learn high-speed driving. At first, it seems as if you don't have time to take any corrective action when you push the vehicle to its limits and it spins out. Yet the more practice laps you take, the more familiar you become with the car operating at its limits. Your perception of time elongates, and before you know it, there's plenty of time to feel what the car's doing beneath you and to input corrections. You become far more self-aware and comfortable operating the vehicle at the edge of the envelope.

Combatives training is the same way. The more you do it, the more you'll find efficiencies that allow you to do things you'd have never thought possible. After a short while, you'll have increased sensitivity,

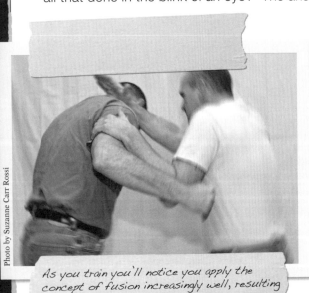

As you train you'll notice you apply the concept of fusion increasingly well, resulting in improved speed and simultaneity.

and everything you do will happen simultaneously. You'll grow increasingly comfortable with someone attacking you. You'll grow increasingly uncomfortable defending. You'll become comfortable in the attack and relentlessly pursue strong finishes.

Keep in mind that it's all worthwhile. Videotape your training. Archive the first couple of week's worth of training tapes. After training regularly once a week for 12 weeks, tape your 12th training session. Go home, sit down with a cold frosty and watch your original tape. Then put in your most recent. I'm pretty sure you'll feel good about what you see.

PART III

COMBATIVES ARE RUTHLESS.

CHAPTER 8
UNARMED SITUATIONAL SELF-OFFENSE

This section of the book includes 10 different scenarios appropriate for the use of combatives on the street. I intentionally mixed up the severity of the situations and the responses to demonstrate various less-violent to violent options. Before we start though, we should review what constitutes the unlawful use of force (re: are you being assaulted?) and the lawful use of pre-emptive force (re: justifiable self-defense).

CRIMINAL USE OF FORCE

The unlawful use of force begins with the threat of violence. It escalates to assault and culminates in battery. The various degrees of assault are defined according to state law, but *generally*, here's what is considered the criminal use of force from a legal perspective:

- **Terroristic threat.** A threat to commit violence communicated with the intent to terrorize another. "I'm gonna bust your ass motherfucker!"

- **Assault.** An unlawful attempt or offer, with force or violence, to do bodily harm to someone, either from ill will or extreme carelessness. For example, a guy takes a swing at you or shakes his fist at you in a threatening or insulting manner. It also constitutes assault if the guy demonstrates the intent to use actual violence coupled with the ability to do so—he opens his knife and slashes the air between the two of you then points it at you.

- **Battery.** Generally, battery is the willful and unlawful use of force or violence on a person, like a guy who snatches a handful of your shirt and yokes you up. It includes the touching or striking of a person against their will. A guy suckers you, for example.

Note: Assault and battery is simply a combination of the two individual crimes in a single incident.

LAWFUL USE OF PRE-EMPTIVE FORCE

Pre-emptive use of force in self defense—in particular lethal force—is generally considered justifiable *only* when your attacker had the ability and opportunity to harm you and caused you to reasonably perceive you were in immediate jeopardy. Let's take a brief look at each of these elements.

- **Ability.** Your attacker was physically able to harm you. Other considerations in establishing that an attacker had the ability to hurt you include whether he was armed or not, if there was a significant disparity in size between you and him and if multiple assailants were present.

- **Opportunity.** He had the opportunity to harm you. This is usually considered relative to his proximity to you. In other words, how far he was from you and whether or not an immediate action taken by him constituted an imminent and harmful situation for you.

- **Jeopardy.** You must have reasonably perceived immediate jeopardy *when you acted*. If you're not in immediate jeopardy, you've no right to either use or continue to use force because you wouldn't be acting in self-defense. For example, you unbalance and knock your attacker down. You'd be justified in using additional force to stop him if he's still able to prevent your escape and still close enough and able to harm you.

- **Pre-emption.** Pre-emptively using force to avoid being harmed is generally considered lawful only if the *totality* of the situation would reasonably result in the perception of being at imminent risk of being harmed.

    The topic of pre-emption is a legal morass and one I'm not willing to trudge through here. It's a virtual Pandora's box filled with vastly differing opinions because, as they say, the law is open to interpretation. Lawyers arguing opposing sides of any case each construct theories based on the same facts and logic, yet somehow they arrive at separate, logical conclusions. Hmmmm. What I'm saying is that the wiggle room inherent in our system of justice, created by interpretation and argument, can either help or hang you.

Suffice it to say, the burden of proof is on you to show your justification for using force pre-emptively. That burden includes articulating your reliance on all the things I've discussed throughout this book to avoid confrontation *and* exercise appropriate restraint.

Like I said, none of this is peel-and-stick easy.

THE SCENARIOS

Scenarios are synopses of hypothetical situations used to make you consider many possible solutions in order to develop a course of action. These thought exercises ultimately influence and optimize your actual performance.

Scenarios only work if you accept the conditions of the scenario. It doesn't matter if the real 3-D "you" wouldn't do what the hypothetical "you" did to get into the situation represented by the scenario; that's not the point. The point is to apply rigor in developing a course of action based solely on the conditions as they're described. Otherwise there wouldn't *be* any scenarios because everyone in 3-D always makes correct choices and successfully avoids difficult and terrible situations—right?

I didn't use third-party scenarios because, frankly, there isn't an easy way to write them without tripping all over personal pronouns or making the whole thing utterly confusing for you to read. Please keep in mind as you read the scenarios my comments aren't critical of you and don't infer the real you made poor choices. I'm merely using a theoretical "you" to more easily create written scenarios.

Scenarios funnel and channel your thoughts by intentionally limiting your choices. This makes you focus on the points the trainer is emphasizing. At this point in the book, it's all about the application of combatives so the omnipresent assumption for all the scenarios is if you could've avoided the situation, you would have.

Scenarios can be frustrating because they make you play the cards you're dealt. Sometimes that means you're holding a shitty hand. The difference between scenarios and real life is that on the street, you can't just fold your hand. You've got to play.

Just as in real life, always consider the following when you construct your course of action:

- the severity of the situation
- the speed with which you must act
- the potential presence of weapons
- unaccounted for hands

Remember, there aren't any guarantees on the street—right? Every situation has too many variables that affect the outcome. Some of these variables are apparent, and some you'll never be aware of. This means there are equally as many possible courses of action. As the idiom goes: "There are lots of ways to skin a cat." The solutions I've included here represent only some of them. My intent is to make you think about the realities of street violence, the application of combatives to prevail and to emphasize the following universal points:

- You should always be armed with a legal less-lethal or lethal weapon.
- *Never* fight empty-handed unless you're forced to.
- The only certainty in violent situations is the presence of uncertainty.
- Bad things *can* happen to good people.
- Attacks with no discernable forewarning do happen and will catch you flatfooted.
- Verbal de-escalation is not always a viable alternative.
- Results are *always* conditional.
- Courage doesn't mean being unafraid; it means remaining proficient despite the presence of fear.
- The successful application of combatives is 90-percent mind-set and 10-percent technique.
- Finally—and unfortunately—sometimes you're just screwed. There isn't an answer for every situation. There isn't always a happy ending. And that fact should make you feel really, really uneasy.

The following hypothetical attacks are based on newspaper accounts of assaults that have occurred across the United States and overseas. Some ended well for the victims, and some ended tragically. Enter the scenario at the point indicated and, by considering *only* the information provided, determine what your best courses of combatives action are. Keep in mind that you never have all the information you'd prefer to have and that ambiguity on the street is extant. Each situation demonstrates how simple and useful combatives are within the use-of-force continuum and includes:

- a short narration that describes the nature and circumstances of the threat
- pre-incident indicators if any exist
- *retrospectively*, actions that may have resulted in avoiding the situation
- any advantages to capitalize on
- a notional response
- a summary including other relevant comments and observations

All right, let's do this.

PISSED OFF IN THE PARKING LOT

Description

You pull into an empty parking space at the local grocery store. As you get out of your car and close your door, a horn sounds behind you. You look in that direction as you hit the lock button on your key chain and see a vehicle quickly stop behind yours. The driver jumps out and looks pissed off. You assume it's about the parking space.

There's no one else in his vehicle. Leaving his car door open, he aggressively advances on you. His jaw is tight, his teeth are bared, and he's muttering something. You profile him for weapons, finding both hands empty. He's got no clip-on knife on either pocket rim and no bulges or printing around his waistline.

You index and start to placate, appease or appeal to him, but he surges forward. Despite backing away from him with your hands up, he's able to snatch a handful of your shirt in one hand. You transition into your guard. He's shouting something really derisive at you. His other hand is drawn back and balled into a fist...

Pre-Incident Indicators

Wow—none, really. Could you have been at fault somehow? Did you unwittingly cut him off to grab the parking space because you were preoccupied? Guess you may never know what set this dude off.

Avoidance Opportunities

If you've unintentionally wronged someone, no matter how slight, at least you've got a useful tool in verbal de-escalation, which is your admission of the unintended slight. Remember, it's not *your* perception of whether you did or didn't slight someone that counts—it's theirs.

The second you recognize there's an issue (before he laid his hands on you), you could at least *try* to verbally de-escalate the situation while you backed away and profiled him for weapons. Watch him closely. Running your mouth is in part a true effort to de-escalate the situation and part ear candy for his benefit. What would you say? How about something like this: "Whoa man! I'm sorry! Did I *not* see you and take your parking spot? Happy to give it up for you. Say the word."

Look, if someone's that outrageously unreasonable and ready to fight over a freakin' parking space, he's got issues. You need to ask yourself, "Am *I* willing to fight over this?" And by the way, that doesn't mean you won't have to even if you're not.

I can't attribute this quote to anyone but I heard it years ago, and it's proven to be the case in my life time and time again: "It's easier to avoid trouble than fight your way out of it." Bail on this red-faced chump now because everything's gonna change once he grabs on...

Available Advantages

Use the environment to your advantage if you can by maneuvering barricades between you and him if that's possible. If the situation gets violent, use the vehicles around you to your advantage.

Immediate Actions: Clavicle Notch

1. You've indexed and are transitioning to your guard just as he shoots his hand forward, snatching your shirt.

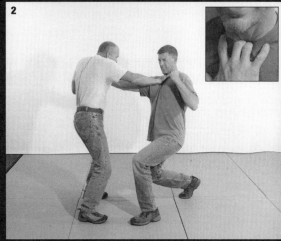

Detail photo by Suzanne Carr Rossi.

2. Hand hook his right hand with your left. Simultaneously jerk him forward by twisting at the waist and moving out of line. Jam your fingers into and then down behind his clavicle notch. Try to tickle his lungs while you maintain pressure with your hand hook.

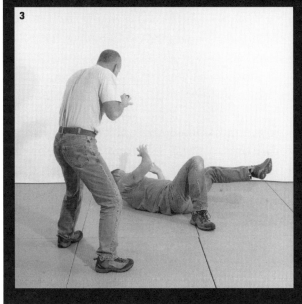

3. Release your hand hook and let him go when you feel him buckling, pulling away and falling to the ground. Recover into your guard, back away and give him verbal commands to leave you alone or stay down. Tell him you're calling the police. Continue to recede, getting further and further away while putting physical barriers between you and him. If you've got a weapon, now would be a good time to discreetly get it out and have it ready but not visible.

Summary

There's no need to brandish your weapon because it may not dissuade this yahoo; instead it may incite him. You're not in immediate jeopardy any longer. Having your weapon ready in case your attacker retrieves a weapon from his vehicle, or just gets up and charges you, is enough.

At this point you need to remove yourself from his line of sight. If you stick around, you're a visible and accessible target for his rage.

As you back away, you notice your hands trembling. Weirdly, you're out of breath, your mouth's dry and you've got to shake your head to clear it. What the hell was *that* all about? Dunno, but good for you! Having profiled him for weapons and being confident he had none, you used the least amount of unarmed force necessary to stop the threat so you could escape. You exercised restraint, limiting your response to avoid really hurting the dope with a face mash or chin jab. Another appropriate alternative would've been a finger jab to stop him and disrupt his vision without creating too much injury.

RAMBUNCTIOUS ROGUE AT THE RESTAURANT

Description

You're leaving a restaurant when you're bumped by a customer (a big dude) who's coming in. There's not a lot of space inside the restaurant vestibule so you turn to say, "Sorry." But the guy who bumped into you is in a rage and grabs your neck with both hands. He slams you against the wall and screams in your face, "Watch where the fuck you're going you *asshole*!" He digs his thumbs into the sides of your windpipe. You can't breathe…

Pre-Incident Indicators

None, sorry.

Avoidance Opportunities

None.

My editor, Sarah Dzida, made the following editorial comment at this point in the original manuscript: "I get why there's nothing left to do but act, but you need to say something more than, 'None.' When I read that in pre-incident indicators then again in avoidance opportunities, I actually was like, 'Seriously?' I even got a little flutter in my stomach."

Good, I'm making my point. Look, shit happens. Not good shit either. These explosive, unexplainable situations transcend any alternative other than instantly using hyperviolence to reverse the confrontational dynamic, period.

What else are you gonna do? Use your best choked-out Donald Duck voice and try verbal de-escalation? Rely on hope? Hope another customer breaks it up? Hope a cop's nearby and responds? Listen, hope's a nice idea but it doesn't *do* anything for you. Hope doesn't belong in a fight. It belongs on bumper stickers and in a haiku.

Available Advantages

Use the wall for support to stay upright and to spring off of. Use it to ram his sack-of-potatoes ass into. When you're able, grab anything in the vestibule you can to use as an improvised weapon. Use anything handy to keep your distance from him—a real-estate magazine rack, someone's umbrella, whatever.

Immediate Actions: Arm Drag Reversal

1. Get your hands up and hand hook his right arm. Jerk it downward—hard. Use the wall and spring your right shoulder off of it, creating momentum. Slam your opposite forearm, using the ulna, down into the crook of his left arm.

2. Your out-of-line movement and arm drag slings the attacker forward into the wall and stuns, but doesn't hurt, him. He's still an active aggressor.

3-4. Chamber and fire some wicked slashing elbows, repeatedly hitting his face and head.

Continued ➜

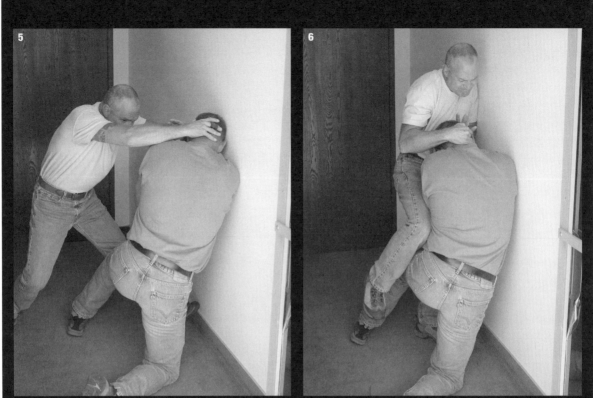

5-6. He's hurt but still trying to get up. Jeeeezus! Grab his head and cycle powerful straight knees into his ribcage, maintaining control of his head. Alternate between elbow and knee strikes (throw in an ankle stomp whenever you can) until he goes slack and quits.

Summary

A two-handed finger choke disrupts both blood and air flow to your brain. It can also damage your larynx and hyoid bone. Death results slowly from a finger choke, but air starvation and the associated panic is immediate and may prevent you from being clearheaded enough to take action if you don't act quickly—besides, why wouldn't you?

You'll probably never know what caused this situation—steroids maybe? Perhaps your attacker was the disgruntled significant other of a waitress he was coming to kill; now *there's* a scary thought. The bottom line is you didn't do anything but were viciously assaulted. Don't waste any more time thinking about it. Strange, unexplained attacks happen every day. Read your local newspaper if you don't believe me.

Undoubtedly, you created quite a ruckus wrangling with the rambunctious rogue at the restaurant. You should separate yourself from the situation and your attacker. Call the police from a position of safety and tell them your current location and the location where the incident occurred. Give them the details and let them deal with any aftermath. If you acted justifiably, you shouldn't be overly concerned that they'll want a statement from you. Be sure to articulate the disparity in size between you and your attacker, that there wasn't any provocation and that you were in fear for your life.

Absolve yourself of any feelings of responsibility to restore order to the restaurant, calm other patrons down or explain your actions to anyone other than the police; you're not the Dalai Lama. It's not uncommon for victims of an explosive situation like this to run their jib nonstop—to anyone who'll listen—as they decompress. Shut your mouth. Don't make any "utterances" that could be overheard and misunderstood or misconstrued by witnesses who may then inaccurately quote you.

The same is true *while* you fight. If you're charged with a crime as a result of your actions, the last thing you need is to have some bystander testify that you were screaming, "I'll fucking *kill* you, you son of a bitch!"

Remember, police officers routinely deal with inexplicable, unprovoked assaults on innocent people. They usually have a well-tempered perspective on these kinds of things. If you have any doubts about how your actions may be considered in hindsight, exercise your Miranda rights and don't say *anything* to the police other than wanting a lawyer with you during questioning or to assist you in preparing your statement. Be courteous and respectful to the police about it because they're just trying to do their job.

THE PERILS OF PARTYING

Description

You attend a party thrown by someone you just met. It's raucous. The music's loud, and people are drunk. You notice a couple of men looking at you, but when you look back at them, they quickly look away. Uneasy, you move to a different place in the party away from them, but a few minutes later, you notice the same guys are now even closer to you. You casually glance at them and one asks, "What the fuck YOU looking at?!" Wisely you just turn to walk away, but another guy blocks your exit. Just as you start to say something to him, you're grabbed from behind in an arm choke and lifted up onto your toes...

Pre-Incident Indicators

There was suspicious nonverbal communication leading up to this situation—the men who evaded eye contact with you despite the fact they initiated it. That kind of behavior could be interpreted as an indication of a hostile collaboration targeting you.

Their movement correlated with yours when you moved out of sight. Worse, it resulted in them getting closer to you than they were initially.

Of course the last pre-incident indicator was the unnatural impediment to your escape when you turned around.

Avoidance Opportunities

On the first uneasy eye contact, you made the right call and drifted to another location out of their line of sight. Out of sight, out of mind—right?

In my opinion, deciding not to just bail was asking for trouble. Faced with this situation, you want to stand wherever you can that restricts direct access to you but also has a ready, unrestricted exit.

You could always join a group. You're much less likely to be attacked in a group and you significantly increase the possibility of someone intervening because there's safety in numbers.

Available Advantages

Identify an improvised weapon and get it in your hand, like beer in a party cup. When you unexpectedly and forcefully throw anything carbonated into someone's eyes, it causes a burning sensation and can cause the eyes to involuntarily slam shut. Rip a beer can in two and you've made two nasty gouging tools. Even glasses when folded closed and held in your hand become an ugly, improvised weapon when you gouge someone's face with the hinged ends where the bows meet the frame. Ugh—but hey! You're never *really* unarmed. You just may not have the stomach to use what's available.

You should also spot any environmental advantages like vertical edges in doorjambs or opened doors, horizontal edges of furniture and shelving that you can use.

Immediate Actions: Standing-Arm Choke Release

1. Throw your hands up and hand hook his forearm, pulling down to relieve the pressure of his choke.

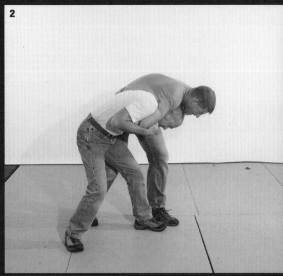

2. Snap down explosively and wrench your shoulders and hips perpendicular to his. Keep pulling his arm down. Violently twist your shoulders within the choke putting unbearable pressure on his chest with the point of your left shoulder.

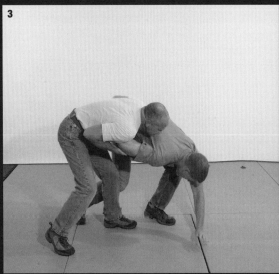

3. Popping your head free, lock his arm and ram him forward, attacking with your body. Force him to the ground and hyperextend his arm.

4. You've chambered the slashing elbow and are ready to drill the base of his skull if he postures up, but don't fire it. He's not resisting anymore. Ask him, "What the fuck are you doing man?"

Summary

Your heart's hammering and you realize you only hear a rush in your ears. You lift your head to get some situational awareness and have to turn your head left and right to see the whole room because you've got tons of spots in your eyes and can't see clearly.

There's a room full of people looking at both of you. A couple guys step forward to break it up and pull you apart. You head to the exit but pull one of the guys who broke the fight up with you. Keep talking to him so he'll stay with you and cover your exit.

The trick now is to skedaddle before the guy whose ass you just kicked hooks up with his shit-starter buddies. Since they undoubtedly colluded to instigate the fight, you don't want to get jammed up outside by the three of them.

You get to your car without incident and leave, stopping off at Taco Bell on the way home to your apartment. While you're waiting in the drive-thru lane, you text tonight's host: <Thanks for a good time. WTF? Nice friends dude. L8R.>

HOTEL HORROR SHOW

Description

You're walking back to your hotel after a meal with your significant other. From a distance, you notice two men sitting on the back of a park bench in the quadrangle you two are traversing. They notice you and stand up. After looking around, they approach you on an oblique angle. Still at a distance, they ask you a question in a language you don't understand. Momentarily, you're perplexed. They look at each other briefly and continue walking toward you. As they enter your immediate space, one punches your girlfriend in the head. The other lunges and grabs you in an overarm bear hug. He lifts you off your feet and starts to slam you to the ground. You catch a glimpse of the other man reaching down toward your girlfriend then dragging her…

Pre-Incident Indicators

The men's sudden change in status when they first noticed you was odd. They went from minding their own business, just sitting on a park bench, to standing and then approaching you. Okay, that was certainly cause for suspicion.

Their intent to intersect your path using an oblique approach and their unsolicited attempt to engage with you should've resulted in some actions taken to avoid them. See below.

Avoidance Opportunities

When you first saw them noticing you, you could've simply turned around and gone back to your point of origin if you felt truly at risk. If you didn't feel that at risk, you could've slowed down or stopped and then assessed what their reaction to *your* sudden change in status was. It'd be wise to stop and loiter near a physical barricade if any were nearby.

Continuing the show (for their consumption), you may have let them notice you sliding a hand inside your coat, where a weapon could be concealed, and leaving it there. You'd assess their reaction to that movement such as stopping and looking at each other. Maybe it's time for them to have a nonverbal discussion about whether they should or shouldn't follow through with their attack or not.

You could've looked at them (not menacingly) and opened your cell phone, leading them to surmise you were ready to call the police. Hell, sometimes just a vocal challenge or warning will dissuade half-assed hooligans.

You'd obviously profile them for weapons—finding their hands, looking for any weapons printing, asking yourself if their movements indicate either scumbag could be concealing a weapon.

If I were you and couldn't just escape, I'd be looking around for anything to use as an improvised weapon. Actually, that's not possible. I couldn't be you because I'D BE ARMED. Lastly, you'd definitely want to position yourself between the threat and your girlfriend, even if that meant a last minute shove to get her out of reach so she could run.

Available Advantages

None. Bet you wish you were armed right now.

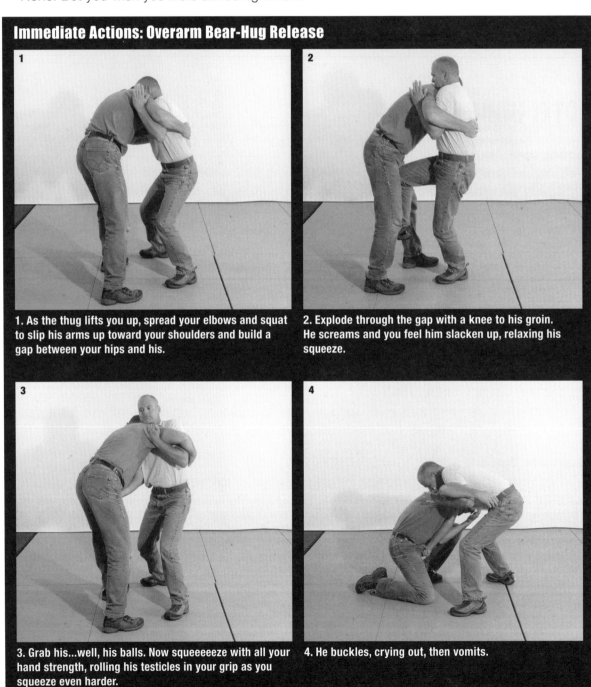

Immediate Actions: Overarm Bear-Hug Release

1. As the thug lifts you up, spread your elbows and squat to slip his arms up toward your shoulders and build a gap between your hips and his.

2. Explode through the gap with a knee to his groin. He screams and you feel him slacken up, relaxing his squeeze.

3. Grab his...well, his balls. Now squeeeeeze with all your hand strength, rolling his testicles in your grip as you squeeze even harder.

4. He buckles, crying out, then vomits.

5. He lets go, and you start to disengage, but he tries to stand. You can't afford for him to recover only to reattack you as you try to help your girlfriend. Or worse, he could continue to hurt your girlfriend while you deal with his partner.

6. Fuck this! Rip as nasty a vicious slashing elbow as you can to his brainstem. Visualize knocking his head right off his neck. He goes limp and face plants.

7. Crush the can on his knee then bolt over to assist your girlfriend.

Summary

These men attacked without provocation or warning indicating a predilection for violence. Self-defense situations are always exponentially more complicated when your responsibility to protect is split between yourself and someone you are responsible for. Unfortunately, criminal predators know this and use it to their advantage.

Everyone's nightmare scenario is to see a loved one hurt or worse to be made to watch helplessly *while* they're hurt. There's no time for emotion in these situations. Take care of business and do it quickly. Here's how this particularly ugly scenario may play out:

You turn and close with the second attacker yelling for help and making as much noise as possible to draw the attention of anyone nearby. Look for a weapon in the second attacker's hand as you close. Don't consider the condition of your girlfriend yet. You need to stop her attacker *first*, so he can't attack you as you're helping her. You can't help her and fight someone off at the same time. You'll do neither adequately.

Look for blood on her indicating she was stabbed or bludgeoned, which would mean there's a weapon in the mix you haven't seen yet. You can't hear anything but your heart thudding in your chest. Yeah, you're hearing your heart thudding.

You're gassed, huffing and wheezing and can't see anything but your girlfriend's attacker, so you sweep your head from side to side to increase your field of vision, looking for any other accomplices or people arriving to intervene and help you.

The other attacker's still doing something violent to your girl although you can't exactly make out what. Using the startle he'll feel when he realizes what's about to happen, you ATTACK him.

THINGS GET HAIRY WAITING FOR HARRY

Description

Standing in line for the latest Harry Potter book, you inadvertently rock back on your heels and crush a little girl's big toe. She screams in terror and pain. You turn around to apologize, but her irate father is already rearing back. With both hands, he tries to shove you backward onto the ground…

Pre-Incident Indicators

None. Shit! The kid's scream startled *you* as much as it did her old man! You were still dealing with that when her dad cooked off on you.

Avoidance Opportunities

Verbal de-escalation of course, and you were saying you were sorry when this guy just attacked you.

Available Advantages

None needed.

Immediate Action: Front Pushing Attack

1. Fend his palm heels up and over your shoulders as he comes in to shove you, then lift your knee. You're not trying to hurt the guy; you're just using your knee to maintain separation between you and him.

2. Keep telling him it was a mistake and that you're sorry. He's probably amped way up and not hearing a word you're saying, but everyone else in line will. He misses the shove and kind of half-assedly tries to grab you around your neck in a finger choke. As you put your foot down, hand hook his left arm and pivot on your left foot, opening the gate. Slam your left forearm across and against the back of his right upper arm, using your ulna.

3. Follow through with a hip and shoulder twist, knocking him away from you and down onto the ground. He falls away— exhausted. His daughter walks over and shin kicks you.

Summary

Whoa!!! Big mistake! BIG MISTAKE!!! You don't want to hurt this guy. He's just reacting to his daughter's shriek—who wouldn't? This is one of those weird quasi-explosive bursts of violence where the right thing to do (once you've controlled your "attacker") is to first close up any gaps between you and him. You don't want him to start thrashing around again. Then, you start apologizing, reassuring and placating the guy you just punked.

Sounds weird, I know. But I've actually been in several of these strange situations in which I've had to apply carefully regulated force to establish control over a big misunderstanding and what appears to be a normally rational person.

You've got to remain vigilant though. My experience in these violent oddities has been that the cool-down period—immediately following the festivities—is made up of waves of emotion. For example, a guy may initially recognize he was out of line and that the whole donnybrook was over a big misunderstanding and be apologetic. Then, after he realizes he got spanked, he may get pissed off that you humiliated him in front of people. Next thing you know, he's actually *thanking you* because he recognizes you exercised restraint and could've fucked him up but didn't.

So make nice and get the hell out of there. It was probably a big deal in the "attacker's" life, making him a real Chatty Cathy…Whoa! LOOK at the time! Have a nice day, gotta run!

Situations like these are awkward, surreal and leave everyone involved feeling kind of weird. Huh.

THE STINKER IN THE STAIRWAY

Description

Leaving work one night, you walk down the stairs that lead to the side exit. You notice someone's propped the door open a crack with a small stone against company security policy. Damn smokers, you think as you reach to push the door open. Suddenly you're attacked from the alcove next to the stairs by someone who must've been hiding there. There isn't much room. You get hit in the head and stumble. Seeing an opportunity, you bury your shoulder into your attacker's gut and reach for his legs to take him down. He sets a guillotine choke and sprawls. You push him backward trying to get to his legs. His feet hit the junction of the wall and floor, and he stops dead—holding the choke and lifting…

Pre-Incident Indicators

Seeing the door propped open, you'd have to assume that access to the building wasn't controlled for an unknown period of time. This could mean unauthorized people are lurking inside.

Avoidance Opportunities

Although humans are creatures of habit and you normally wouldn't even slow down on your way out the door, you should. A little caution goes a long way. Put on your predator hat. If you were a mugger that didn't want to get too deep inside a building and subject yourself to being challenged, where would *you* stand to mug someone? Look there before you commit to the stairwell.

Available Advantages

Nope.

Immediate Actions: Standing Guillotine Reversal

1. Caught off guard, you just drive forward, which just makes the choke tighter as the attacker straightens up. Reach up and use a left hand hook on his right forearm to relieve some pressure from the choke.

2. Your attacker's grunting and trying to squeeze the choke tighter. GOD! He STINKS! Twist your head inward, nose to his center, to get his forearm off your windpipe. Whip your right elbow up, clearing his head and twisting your torso to load your strike.

3. Violently slam the crook of your arm down onto the back of his neck to stun him and rotate his head through with the strike. He reaches to the ground to try and stay on his feet, abandoning his choke on you. I mean he REALLY smells bad!

4. Drive your forearm further through its arc, twisting your attacker's upper body. Keep your forearm on the side of his neck and pull upward, keeping his head tight to your chest. You think, "I really, hope this creep doesn't have lice…" Now that you've reversed him, what the hell do you do?

Summary

That you were attacked in a confined space by someone who secreted themselves from view indicates real predatory behavior. The chance of either someone happening onto the situation and intervening or of hearing your calls for help are minimal. Any unskilled person who applies a choke or neck manipulation has to be dealt with swiftly because of the high likelihood of you getting a neck injury.

Since you had exploited forward movement to the limit of advance by backing him against the wall, he has no choice other than to choke you harder or manipulate your neck to the point of permanent injury. You've got no time to spare and have to act quickly to avoid being choked out or seriously injured.

Hold on a minute. Hmmm. Why'd you drive forward initially anyway? Probably seemed like the thing to do at the time. Duress has a funny way of making logic fuzzy. As you learned in Chapter 4, your ability to branch quickly from a failed technique to another is critical to maintaining your momentum.

And why did I leave you hanging at the end of that scenario? Because I wanted you to think, that's why. So here's your problem: You've used some ground skills in that you reversed his guillotine and got a vicious neck crank on your attacker. Now what? This is when the *Jeopardy!* theme song plays. I doubt your attacker knows what tapping out is. Even if he did, then what? The guy who just assaulted you taps out and suddenly agrees to let you go? Okay, that's no help.

Your neck crank only has one level to escalate to after pain and that's causing serious neck injury. Do you go for it? In light of everything you know now about the use of force, do you snap his neck? I didn't think so. So that's not a good answer.

Hey wait a minute—you don't know whether or not he's got a weapon and you can't keep his hands from drawing one if he does. So *that's* a problem.

What's a major strength of combatives? Simplicity, right? Release your neck crank and let go of him. Grab his filthy head and throw some knees into his face from below and finish the smelly bastard with some hammerfists from above.

When you think simply and brutally, there always seems to be an answer. Whenever I'm confronted with students who can't help themselves from blurting out ridiculous and endless "what if" variations of attacks, my response is always the same. "Don't present it to me in the form of a question. Don't tell me what you're going to do. Come out here and do it to me. But understand the default answer in combatives is always more power, more pain." You see, combatives really are *that* simple. You should never find you've been stymied, not for a second.

TERROR IN THE TOILET

Description

You jump into a public restroom to relieve yourself. No one else is inside. You hear the door open behind you as you walk to the line of urinals, and two young men walk in following in trace. As they overtake you, one says, " 'scuse me," to ask you something. The other continues past you to the urinals. You're turning to face the man asking the question when suddenly you're seized from behind in a double arm lock.

Pre-Incident Indicators

Any pre-incident indicators would have been visible outside of the restroom. The thugs were so close behind you, they must have been following you or they were loitering around the bathroom observing who went in.

Avoidance Opportunities

None.

Available Advantages

None.

Immediate Actions: Rear Double Arm-Lock Escape

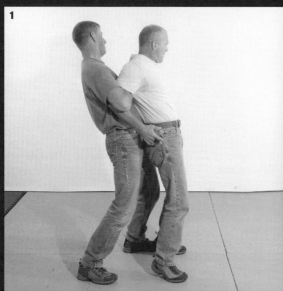

1. Startled at first, you lean forward against the pressure of the arm lock. That only bends your arms at the elbows. This actually makes it easier for the thug behind you to hold on and more impossible for you to get out.

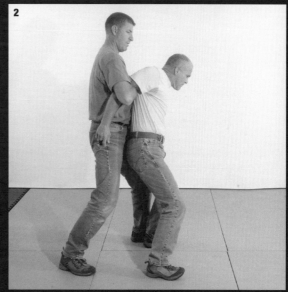

2. Completely relax your right arm and crouch slightly, dropping your weight. With your arm relaxed, the thug won't be able to tighten his hold on your right arm enough to hold it.

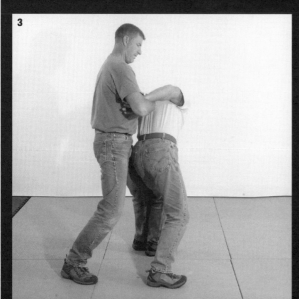

3. Leave your left arm tense and slightly bent. You're going to make it a fulcrum. Violently shrug your right shoulder forward and slide your right arm free as you pivot on your left foot.

4. The speed of your movement and ease with which you escaped an apparently secure hold catches both thugs off guard.

Continued ▶

5. Transition your tense and slightly bent left arm into an arm lock as you whip a right hammerfist all the way around...

Ba.

Boom.

6. ...and into the base of the thug's skull who was holding you a second ago and then...

7. ...transition to an armbar forcing him to the ground.

Summary

You're on the other side of the unconscious miscreant who grabbed you. You're armed today—surprise! So you draw and open your folder and close with the second thug. You shout, "Go on, get the fuck outta here!" He turns and runs out of the bathroom.

It's time again for my editor, Sarah, to piss on my perfectly good parade. Here are her questions about this scenario's ending:

- *"What if he doesn't run?"* I don't care if he runs or he doesn't. The most important thing is that, with my knife out, the second guy can't keep *me* from running out of there. And yes, if he tries to impede my escape, I'll use the knife to slash and thrust my way to safety.
- *"Do you want to finish the first guy so violently and quickly because you don't know what the second will do?"* I only have two speeds—on and off. I've only got two levels of violence—some of it and all of it. As I said earlier in the book, *always* move explosively, but regulate your force based on what's appropriate for the point you enter the force continuum, remember? In regard to a multiple-assailant situation where weapons may be present (we never did get to profile the thugs…), they get the *all*-violence option.
- *"Do you need to remain aware of him?"* Of course I want to remain aware of the second attacker and I have to assume he'll try to help his buddy—I would, wouldn't you?
- *"If he runs, do you or don't you go after him?"* If he runs out of the restroom, I'm running after him. Not because I want to catch him, cut him or execute a citizen's arrest. I'll run out after him in order to keep track of him as I escape, so he doesn't disappear only to reappear with a weapon or reinforcements.
- *"If he stays, do you need to take him down with the same violence as the first or just enough to immobilize him?"* Just because I dropped some thug who was robbing me doesn't mean I have any responsibility more urgent than my own to get to safety. Why the hell would I stay there anyway? To take my leak? Too late. I probably pissed all over myself in the middle of this fracas anyway.

Actually I'd understand if the second thug wanted to stay. I wouldn't leave a friend lying unconscious on a piss-stained floor in a public restroom either. Either way, if he stays or he doesn't, I don't care because *I'm* leaving.

SURVIVING ON A SHOESTRING

Description
You and some professional colleagues are walking to a restaurant from your hotel after a full day of business. You inadvertently step on your shoelace and it comes untied. You stop to retie it and tell your workmates you'll catch up in a second. As you bend down to tie your shoe, you hear several popping noises, and weirdly when you look up, two of your colleagues are laying on the sidewalk with a man bent over them. "What the fuck?" you ask yourself and stand up quickly. They weren't just shot. Were they? A gun is thrust into your back and you hear, "Don't move motherfucker…"

Pre-Incident Indicators
None.

Avoidance Opportunities
None.

Available Advantages
None.

Immediate Actions: Pistol Rear

1. Oh my God…Put your arms in the air and take a quick glance over your shoulder to see what you'll turn into.

2. Wheel to your left, sweeping your left foot back, clearing your body of the weapon's line of attack (the muzzle).

3. Get your left arm over the top of the pistol and start your chin jab with your right.

4. Tighten your hand around the attacker's arm above his elbow. Lock his arm down. Slam the chin jab home. Visualize his head popping off.

5. As his hip shoots forward, rifle your knee deep into his groin. If he needs another chin-jab knee sequence, let it rip.

Summary

He drops like a stone. Take control of his weapon and make sure he doesn't have another. Check the condition of the weapon to see if it's loaded. You look up and see the other criminal has fled, leaving only your wounded and dead colleagues lying on the sidewalk. You need to call 911 while you check your colleagues' vitals, rendering whatever first aid you're able to until help arrives. Their lives are more important than the criminals and seconds count when gunshot wounds are involved. Do the best you can to provide first aid, keep the unconscious attacker accounted for and wait for the police.

I've sat through classes over my career where scenarios such as this one are explained for hours in excruciating detail. You know what? Alone, under duress, with only one set of hands, having to perform lifesaving procedures when surrounded by dead and wounded friends AND keep an eye on an unconscious murderer, you do the best you can. That's all you can do, just don't fold.

BRICK VS. BLACKBERRY

Description

You park next to a large electrical utilities box even though you know better, but hey! You were in a rush and didn't see any other parking spaces. You get out of the car, lock it and start walking away when you're BlackBerry rings. Damn! Can you not get *even a minute* to run a freakin' errand without someone calling? Something moves to your left so…HOLY SHIT! A guy is swinging something at your head!

Pre-Incident Indicators

You know…you deserve to get hit. You know better than to park near something where someone can secrete themselves. You know better than to have your head down dinking with your BlackBerry or texting when you're on the street. *Especially* given where you parked!

Avoidance Opportunities

There are lots of them but primarily, if you hadn't been preoccupied with your DingleBerry, you wouldn't have been surprised by this attack. If you hadn't been in such a rush, you wouldn't have parked where you did.

Available Advantages

Environmental advantages created by the vehicles as discussed in Chapter 6.

Immediate Actions: Beat Down Reversal

1. You don't even notice the knucklehead with the brick until he's too close.

2. You wheel to face him and see he's got something in his hand coming down toward your head.

3. Vault to get inside the brick, clearing your body of the weapon's line of attack. Bury your shoulder into his gut and knock the wind out of him.

4. Pull inward with your left hand at the small of his back, creating a fulcrum. Using his centerline as a guide, slam your right-handed chin jab into his chin.

5. Keep your left hand in place as a check and drive his head back as far as your range of motion allows.

6. He's hurt but trying to get up. Grab his head and make good use of environmental advantages. Trap him against the vehicle to maximize your…

7.... knee...

8....and elbow sequences to finish him.

Summary

You take off, wondering, "What the fuck did I do with my phone?" You were going to call 911. Patting down your pockets, you notice your hands are shaking—like really shaking. You know better than to allow convenience to outweigh security. Good security is *always* inconvenient. Predators rely on humans erring on the side of convenience in order to choose their attack sites.

Anytime you're attacked without provocation—*especially* with a weapon, *especially* when the weapon's not just being brandished but actually used—the situation is especially serious. Blatant predatorial behavior like that indicates complete disregard for any legal consequence or the victim's well-being. The attacker in this scenario had the ability and the opportunity to harm you, and you rightfully perceived your life was in jeopardy. Act ruthlessly and without hesitation.

RUINS RUBICON

Description

Traveling in a foreign country, you decide to take a local bus to visit some ruins. It's hot. The trip out to the site is along a rural route on rutted secondary roads. As your bus rounds a corner, two bandits flag it down and the bus stops. There are only a few local passengers left on the bus with you. One of the bandits brandishes a pistol as he climbs onto the bus and orders everyone off. The driver protests and gets pistol-whipped by the gunman for his trouble. He's yanked out of his seat and thrown down the steps and out the door, landing unceremoniously on the ground at the feet of the second bandit. The driver's sobbing. The frightened passengers file past the gunman out the door and are kept watch over by the bandit outside the bus. The gunman eyes you and mutters, "*gringo,*" with obvious disdain. He smiles slyly, grips the pistol in both hands and points it at your chest. You look outside and see the unarmed bandit laughing as he watches his partner screw with you.

Pre-Incident Indicators

Did you check the State Department travel advisories? Did you check with the local U.S. embassy when you got in country to get the skinny on local crime trends? Oh yeah, the last pre-incident indicator: YOU'RE ON A REMOTE BACKROAD IN THE THIRD WORLD.

Avoidance Opportunities

You can make an attempt at using guile and wit to run your mouth, but you need to understand that people get killed in remote areas of Central and South America all the time with virtually no consequences. They simply disappear.

Available Advantages

None.

Immediate Actions: Pistol Front

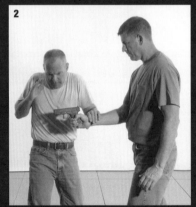

1. You're fighting denial. You're voice is quavering. Your hands are shaking, and you can't believe you were stupid enough to even get into this situation. You know this guy is going to shoot you. Put your hands up and as close to the pistol as the gunman lets you.

2. Jerk your right shoulder back and sweep your right foot back at the same time you "grab" the gunman's arm with your left hand to push it away. "BANG!" He startled and squeezed the trigger, but you're out of the weapon's line of attack and aren't hit.

3. Pull the side of the pistol back into your chest with your left hand as you reach under it with your right and lock onto it. Trapped this way, the gunman can't reorient it back on you. You're behind the muzzle.

4. Using the leverage afforded by your grip on the slide, snap your hips to the left as you spin the pistol within his grip and show him the muzzle. Even with two hands, he can't hang on.

5. Hack down on this little shit's arm with your ulna and jerk the pistol free. You're scared and pissed off and can't help planting the pistol in his face, knocking him—and two of his teeth—out.

Summary

The bus passengers turn on the other bandit and beat him on the side of the road. You learn the next day, they had actually beaten him to death. You thought your trip to the ruins sucked.

—⟋⟋⟋—

You know…if these scenarios were just total fabrications, it might be easy to dismiss them and find some false comfort in a safe and delusional understanding of what actual street violence looks like. Except they're not complete fabrications. Violent episodes like this happen every day—including today, the day you read these words.

Some are outrageous, some are weird, many are forgotten as quickly as they happened (except by the victims or their families), and most end up just as data points in the FBI's annual Uniform Crime Report.

The next time you're shaving in the morning or having your first cup of coffee and listening to the news, do me a favor. When you hear an account of a local murder, rape or robbery, stop what you're doing, sit down and listen. Then think about what you heard in terms of a similar event's impact on your own family. Think about the terror, pain and suffering of the victim during the crime, and if he or she survived, the inevitable diminishment.

Then I'd like you to commit to taking the steps necessary to reduce the likelihood of anything that foul ever happening to you or your loved ones.

Deal?

AFTERWORD

Thanks for reading my book. I appreciate you for tolerating me. I thought it would be appropriate to end the book by drawing corollaries between warfighting and personal combat. Just as any true martial artist should read Musashi's *The Book of Five Rings*, any combatives practitioner should read the U.S. Marine Corps Field Manual 1 (FM 1) *Warfighting*.

It was written in the late 1980s at the Marine Air Ground Task Force Warfighting Center in Quantico, Virginia while I was assigned there to the Special Operations/Low Intensity Conflict office as the Counterterrorism/Counternarcotics Officer. A young Captain, John Sullivan, was a contemporary of mine and a Project Officer on the development of FM 1. The book was written with direct input from the Commandant of the Marine Corps, General A.M. Gray. Through John, I had the opportunity to review it as a work in progress, and it left a lasting impression.

I'll leave you with some of the most applicable corollaries:

WAR

FM 1: *"War is a violent clash of interests between two hostile, independent, and irreconcilable wills, each trying to impose itself on the other."*
Combatives Corollary: There isn't an alternative to violence left.

FM 1: *"It is critical to keep in mind that the enemy is not an inanimate object to be acted upon but an independent and animate force with its own objectives and plans."*
Combatives Corollary: Train with an active partner and not someone who's robotic or remains fixed in place while you execute a technique. Never allow the use of staged pillar assaults to support your technique. Encourage your partner to move freely because your attacker will.

FM 1: *"The object of war is to impose our will on our enemy."*
Combatives Corollary: Ditto.

FRICTION

FM 1: *"Friction is the force that makes the apparently easy so difficult."*
Combatives Corollary: No technique works on the street as easily as it does in training.

FM 1: *"Friction is the force that resists all action and saps energy."*
Combatives Corollary: Fighting for your life saps your strength much more quickly than training or competing does.

FM 1: *"Friction may be mental, as in indecision over a course of action."*
Combatives Corollary: Don't learn too many alternative techniques because it will only result in indecisiveness under duress and increase your reaction time. See Hick's Law.

FM 1: ***"Friction may be self-induced, caused by such factors as lack of a clearly defined goal [...] unclear or complicated plan."***
Combatives Corollary: Rely on your index position to trigger your commitment to attacking. Visualize your plan of action. Keep your techniques brutally simple.

FM 1: ***"While we should attempt to minimize self-induced friction, the greater requirement is to fight effectively despite the existence of friction. One essential means to overcome friction is the will; we prevail over friction through persistent strength of mind and spirit."***
Combatives Corollary: Your sheer will to prevail is unequivocal and a core characteristic of combatives.

UNCERTAINTY

FM 1: ***"The very nature of war makes certainty impossible; all actions in war [are] based on incomplete, inaccurate, or even contradictory information."***
Combatives Corollary: You'll never have all the information you'd like to have before needing to act except in the most obvious attacks.

FM 1: ***"We can learn to fight effectively despite it [uncertainty] by developing simple, flexible plans; planning for likely contingencies and fostering initiative."***
Combatives Corollary: Avoid complex or intricate techniques. Take the initiative when warranted and pre-emptively attack. Strike unexpectedly or in an unexpected way. If a technique fails, immediately branch and explode into another. As quickly as you recognize them, exploit new targets of opportunity.

FM 1: ***"One important source of uncertainty is a property known as nonlinearity [...] minor incidents or actions can have decisive effects."***
Combatives Corollary: An innocuous action taken early in a confrontation can completely change its outcome. Use pre-emption, incidental striking and your environment to give you the decisive advantage.

FM 1: ***"Risk is equally common to action or inaction."***
Combatives Corollary: You must risk being hurt in order to hurt. As an attack gestates, you're at risk if you use violence *and* if you don't.

FM 1: ***"Part of uncertainty is the ungovernable element of chance. Chance is a universal characteristic of war and a continuous source of friction."***
Combatives Corollary: You can do everything correctly and still lose if only by chance. Remember that your attacker may have the advantage and also lose. Since you can't account for chance, don't worry over it. Focus on influencing chance by creating your own advantages.

FM 1: *"The constant potential for chance to influence outcomes in war, combined with the inability to prevent chance from impacting on plans and actions, creates psychological friction [...] However, we should remember that chance favors neither belligerent exclusively."*

Combatives Corollary: Seek every advantage to prevail. Never fight fairly because there's no such thing. Never give an attacker a break. If you do, you may not live to regret it.

FLUIDITY

FM 1: *"Each episode in war is the temporary result of a unique combination of circumstances, presenting a unique set of problems and requiring an original solution."*

Combatives Corollary: Any action you take in a confrontation can result in near infinite reactions. Each reaction is a momentary and unique opportunity you can exploit to defeat your attacker.

FM 1: *"Since war is a fluid phenomenon, its conduct requires flexibility of thought."*

Combatives Corollary: Rage with reason. Keep your wits about you in order to see then exploit the fleeting opportunities discussed above. Stay flexible in the attack. Rely on your rapid-targeting thought process and quickly branch from one technique to another, exploiting opportunities as quickly as they present themselves to overwhelm your attacker.

DISORDER

FM 1: *"As the situation changes continuously, we are forced to improvise again and again until finally our actions have little, if any, resemblance to the original scheme."*

Combatives Corollary: There's a saying in the military: "No operations order survives the first shot." Similarly, no *kata* survives the first punch. Faced with disorder, establish order with overwhelming ferocity. Once you have the momentum, stay on your toes and keep your attacker backing up on his heels. Ruthlessly and relentlessly close with and *finish* him.

THE HUMAN FACTOR

FM 1: *"Since war is an act of violence based on irreconcilable disagreement, it will invariably inflame and be shaped by human emotions."*

Combatives Corollary: Channel your rage but rely on your training.

VIOLENCE AND DANGER

FM 1: "Violence is an essential element of war and its immediate result is blood-shed, destruction, and suffering. While the magnitude of violence may vary with the object and means of war, the violent essence of war will never change. Any study of war that neglects this basic truth is misleading and incomplete."

Combatives Corollary: Your primary goal is to avoid, your secondary goal is to escape unharmed. Unfortunately, depending on the severity of the situation, sometimes it will be necessary to seriously injure or perhaps kill an assailant in order to prevail. For that reason you must never confuse combatives with a "Gentle Art."

ABOUT THE AUTHOR

Kelly McCann is a combatives instructor with over 25 years of experience, a former CNN Security Analyst and founder, as well as president, of Crucible, a high-risk environment training provider that services Department of Defense special-missions units and intelligence and federal law-enforcement agencies. A former U.S. Marine, McCann is the creator of many special-operations tactics, techniques and procedures. He is also the former personal security editor at *Guns & Ammo* and the personality behind several best-selling instructional video/DVDs—all done under the pen name of "Jim Grover." Visit his Web site at www.kellymccanncombatives.com.

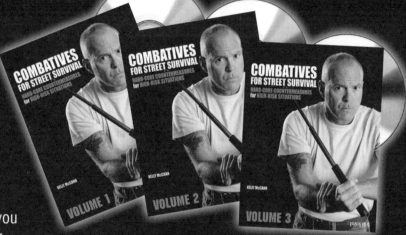

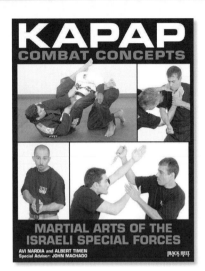
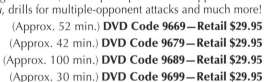
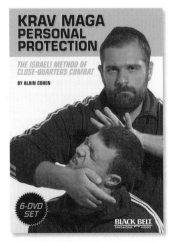

BOOKS AND DVDs FROM BLACK BELT®

BRUCE LEE'S FIGHTING METHOD:
The Complete Edition
by Bruce Lee and M. Uyehara

Bruce Lee's Fighting Method: The Complete Edition brings the iconic four-volume *Fighting Method* series together into one definitive book. Intended as an instructional document to complement Lee's foundational *Tao of Jeet Kune Do*, this restored and enhanced edition of *Fighting Method* breathes new life into hallowed pages with digitally remastered photography and a painstakingly refurbished interior design for improved instructional clarity. This 492-page hard-bound book also includes 900+ digitally enhanced images, newly discovered photographs from Lee's personal files, a new chapter on the Five Ways of Attack penned by famed first-generation student Ted Wong, and an analytical introduction by Shannon Lee that helps readers contextualize the revisions and upgrades implemented for this special presentation of her father's work. 492 pgs. Size 7" x 10".
(ISBN-13: 978-0-89750-170-5) **Book Code 494—Retail $34.95**

CHINESE GUNG FU:
The Philosophical Art of Self-Defense
(Revised and Updated)
by Bruce Lee

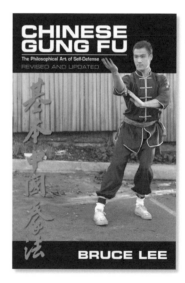

Black Belt Books' new edition of *Chinese Gung Fu: The Philosophical Art of Self-Defense* gives martial arts enthusiasts and collectors exactly what they want: more Bruce Lee. In addition to the master's insightful explanations on *gung fu*, this sleek book features digitally enhanced photography, previously unpublished pictures with Lee's original handwritten notes, a brand-new front and back cover, and introductions by widow Linda Lee Cadwell and daughter Shannon Lee. Fully illustrated. 112 pgs. (ISBN-13: 978-0-89750-112-5)
Book Code 451—Retail $12.95

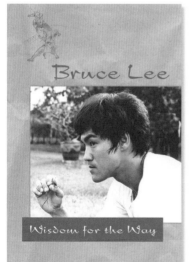

Bruce Lee:
Wisdom for the Way
by Bruce Lee

Wisdom for the Way gives readers direct access to Bruce Lee's thoughts. It pulls from many of Bruce Lee's sources—quotes, pictures, sketches—to create a visually comprehensive reference to the master. The book is also the perfect gift for martial arts enthusiasts, collectors and philosophers who want insight into the mind of Bruce Lee in a compact presentation.
144 full-color pgs. (ISBN-13: 978-0-89750-185-9)
Book Code 491—Retail $15.95

To order, call (800) 581-5222 or visit blackbeltmag.com/shop

BOOKS AND DVDs FROM BLACK BELT®

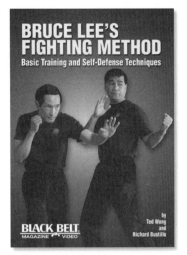

BRUCE LEE'S FIGHTING METHOD: Basic Training and Self-Defense Techniques
by Ted Wong and Richard Bustillo

Bruce Lee's *jeet kune do*, as explained in the book series *Bruce Lee's Fighting Method*. This video covers the first two volumes, with topics including warm-ups, basic exercises, on-guard position, footwork, power/speed training and self-defense. (Approx. 55 min.)
DVD Code 1029—Retail $29.95

The Complete Michael D. Echanis collection
by Michael D. Echanis

This is a comprehensive compilation of the highly popular three-volume *Special Tactics* series from legendary soldier Michael D. Echanis. Since the series first hit the martial arts scene in 1977, Echanis' unique approach to hand-to-hand combat has revolutionized reality-based fighting. 452 pgs. (ISBN: 978-0-89750-197-2)
Book Code 519—Retail $29.95

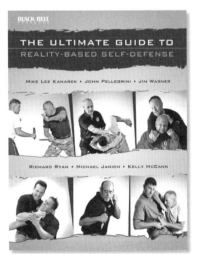

The Ultimate Guide to Reality-Based Self-Defense
by the Editors of Black Belt

Featuring some of the best self-defense articles from the *Black Belt* archives, this book explores a wide spectrum of violent situations, delves into the criminal mind, and teaches you how to effectively assess a violent situation and act accordingly. 128 pgs. (ISBN: 978-0-89750-196-5)
Book Code 515—Retail $21.95

To order, call (800) 581-5222 or visit blackbeltmag.com/shop

VIDEOS FROM BLACK BELT®

Check out
blackbeltmag.com/videos
to see behind-the-scenes footage of our most popular authors, martial artists and MMA fighters!

REVIEWS

"McCann has kept his hands dirty for the 28 years I've known him, staying in the fight and has served, as warriors do. This book contains his direct, unflinching opinions about close combat, and he ought to know."

—General A.M. Gray, former Commandant of the Marine Corps; former member of the Joint Chiefs of Staff; and a current member of the Potomac Institute for Policy Studies, Washington, D.C.

"If you're serious about self-defense, don't settle for theory. Buy this book and get the real deal."

—Michael Janich, founder of Martial Blade Concepts

"Kelly McCann's combatives mentality is as honest and straightforward as it can get."

—Pat Miletich, five-time UFC champion with 14 years of experience training police and military forces

"Kelly McCann approaches the study of combatives from a scientifically based model of 'what and why,' but does so with an almost religious fervor to find the 'best way.' "

—Jim McDonnell, Chief of Staff and Medal of Valor recipient, Los Angeles Police Department

"Kelly McCann is probably the toughest person I know, and one of the smartest. Both qualities are on display in this terrific book, which is not only wise and useful but a compelling read."

—Tucker Carlson, host, MSNBC's Tucker; co-host, CNN's Crossfire

"Kelly McCann's approach to combatives works because it embodies two basic principles: simplicity and proven effectiveness."

—L.H. "Bucky" Burress, Lieutenant Colonel U.S. Army (retired), SFOD-D co-founder

"Kelly was one of the driving forces in updating [and making the] old close combat program [...] fully functional on the modern-day battlefield."

—Cardo V. Urso, former chief trainer, Marine Corps Close Combat Program

"Kelly's understanding of close [and] sudden violence is derived from personal experience."

—Bill Bratton